Education and Development

Education and Development

Policy Imperatives for Jamaica and the Caribbean

CANUTE S. THOMPSON

The University of the West Indies Press
Jamaica • Barbados • Trinidad and Tobago

The University of the West Indies Press
7A Gibraltar Hall Road, Mona
Kingston 7, Jamaica
www.uwipress.com

A catalogue record of this book is available from the National Library
of Jamaica.

ISBN: 978-976-640-777-3 (paper)
978-976-640-778-0 (Kindle)
978-976-640-779-7 (ePub)

Cover design by Robert Harris

Printed in the United States of America

To my wife and children

Contents

Foreword / ix

Acknowledgements / xi

List of Abbreviations / xiii

Introduction / 1

Part 1. Issues in Higher Education

1. Higher Education in the Caribbean and the Challenge of Global Competition / 13

2. Financing Higher Education / 34

Part 2. Social Activism, Economic Development, Crime

3. Social Activism and the Development of the Caribbean / 47

4. Sustainable Economic Development: The Centrality of Education / 55

5. The Anatomy of Crime: A Jamaican Case Study / 70

Part 3. Leadership and Institutional Development

6. Leadership Development: Caribbean Political Leadership in the Spotlight / 89

7. Public Trust / 96

8. Public-Sector Transformation / 104

9. Courageous Leadership: An Appeal / 118

References / 125

Index / 137

Foreword

This book represents an expansion and fine-tuning of some of the public commentaries on issues which the author, Dr C.S. Thompson, has made in recent years via newspaper columns, which I have been reading since the 2000s. These pieces have been well researched, refreshing and relevant. This book, then, is timely and welcomed, as it serves as an easy reference for exploring ideas on a variety of subjects related to regional and national development. Dr Thompson, in this, his sixth book, seeks to explore dimensions of various policy issues from the perspective of the need to radically review how countries of the Caribbean approach socio-economic development in a globalized world. To the same end, it also considers values such as citizen empowerment, public-sector transformation and the management of social ills such as corruption and crime. His objective is to influence public opinion and spur policy action at the political and institutional levels. While there are differences in some of the causes and manifestations of issues facing Caribbean countries, there is a degree of commonality. Thompson seeks to explore those common issues, even while focusing on manifestations in a specific country, Jamaica, with a view to highlighting probable solutions.

The subdivision of the book into sections focusing on (1) issues in higher education; (2) social activism, economic development, crime; and (3) leadership and institutional development provides the reader with a helpful guide on how to navigate the material. Depending on a reader's interest, he or she may select any section of the book and explore the material there. The chapter titles are also quite apt and lend to easy decision-making for the reader concerning an area of study for further information and insight.

Part 1 of the book covers chapters 1 and 2. In chapter 1, Dr Thompson expands on a paper he presented at the Schools of Education Biennial Conference held in Trinidad and Tobago in 2019. In this chapter, he shows the challenges to the University of the West Indies (UWI) competing in a global educational context. He also makes the insightful observation that students move from lesser developed to more developed countries to study, while, on the other hand, developed countries move to lesser developed countries to provide education. Therefore, the money moves from lesser developed to more developed countries. He argues that the UWI and other universities in the

Caribbean region need to adapt their delivery operations to take account of the growing market for studying abroad, which will mean investing heavily in online learning options. The author's arguments outline the catalytic position in which the UWI finds itself and the work that this noble institution needs to do to remain locally competitive and globally relevant.

Chapter 2 discusses models for financing tertiary education. This is a subject of extreme importance given the relationship between tertiary education and sustainable economic growth and development. The author offers some interesting ideas on how countries of the Caribbean may approach the financing of this sector, which deserve due considerations of our policymakers.

Part 2 of the book, chapters 3 through 5, deals with the issues of social activism, productivity, economic growth and development, and crime. In chapter 4, Dr Thompson addresses the issues of activism and social consciousness. It speaks to colleagues in academia and challenges that community to be more visionary and courageous in how they see their roles as academics and social engineers. Chapters 4 and 5 address the issues of economic growth and development (chapter 4) and crime (chapter 5). The discussion of these issues is located within the Jamaican context. Addressing these in the same section is quite appropriate given the impact of crime on economic growth and development in Jamaica. While these issues are explored within the context of Jamaica, they are relevant to the Caribbean, where the levels of violence per capita are excessively high. The problem of violent crimes not only retards economic growth but limits the prospects for sustainable economic development.

Part 3 of the book (chapters 6 through 9) deals with issues of leadership development, fighting corruption and public-sector transformation. Each of these issues represents an area of challenge for countries of the Caribbean, and the author's ideas represent a valuable contribution to matters which must move from discussion to resolute policy action.

This book is a welcomed and unique addition to the material on education and development in the Caribbean and may be the first of its kind with this scope of information. It will be a helpful reference for political practitioners in their role as agents of development and policymaking, as well as to leaders in academia and social policy. It should, of course, become required reading for students in the social sciences.

The Most Honourable Percival James Patterson, ON, OCC, PC, QC
Former prime minister of Jamaica, 1992–2006
President, Heisconsults
9 October 2019

Acknowledgements

I am indebted to many persons whose encouragement, support, feedback and critique have led to the publication of this book. First, I wish to thank the *Jamaica Observer* newspaper for the publications and resultant exposure of many of the ideas on which I have developed in this book and the many readers for their criticisms, questions and feedback.

Second, I wish to thank my brother, Dr Paul Thompson, who read the initial draft of the manuscript and offered helpful suggestions. I also extend a very special thanks and salute to my colleague, Dr Ann-Marie Wilmot, who reviewed a later version of the manuscript and offered exceedingly helpful advice, comments and critique. The thoroughness with which Dr Wilmot reviewed the manuscript was simply of a high standard. My unending thanks also go to my indefatigable research assistants, Nickoda Worghs and Allison Montgomery, for their diligence and professionalism.

Third, I extend profound gratitude to the former prime minister of Jamaica, the Most Honourable P.J. Patterson, for writing the foreword to the book. The esteem with which the most honourable former prime minister is held globally and regionally provides a welcome support and endorsement for this publication. The worth and weight of his contribution cannot be overstated.

Fourth, I must record my debt of gratitude to the University of the West Indies Press for undertaking this second publication, which represents my sixth overall. The partnership with the University of the West Indies Press, which began with my fifth book, has been one of tremendous joy and growth, and I wish to thank the blind peer reviewers for their dedication and thoroughness in the review of the manuscripts. Their approach to the task of review validates my belief that the eighth wonder of the world (and the first beauty of academic publishing) is the "dedicated blind peer reviewer".

Finally, I am grateful for the forbearance of my wife Mauleen, who despite her occasional uneasiness with my public commentaries, has made the conscious decision to be supportive of my efforts in public service and advocacy. I am also grateful to our three children, Orville, Grace-Ann and Janiel, who offer their loving counsel and constant encouragement and who also support my attempts to inform and influence public discourse, despite their apprehensions about and anxieties for my personal safety. I dedicate this book to them.

Abbreviations

CaPRI	Caribbean Policy Research Institute
CPIC	Corruption Prevention and Integrity Commission
GATS	General Agreement on Trade in Services
GDP	gross domestic product
HEI	higher education institution
IDT	Industrial Disputes Tribunal
JTA	Jamaica Teachers' Association
LEGS	Learning, Earning, Giving Back and Saving
NCB	National Commercial Bank
OECD	Organisation for Economic Co-operation and Development
TOJ	Telecommunications of Jamaica
UTECH	University of Technology
UWI	The University of the West Indies

Introduction

This book examines a variety of social and economic issues which affect Jamaica and the Caribbean, and which therefore require attention to mitigate their actual or potential dangers or to grasp the apparent opportunities. The book discusses offerings of some of the policy actions which may be taken in response to these realities and addresses subjects such as education, leadership and institutional development, productivity, economic growth and development, and crime. Some of these ideas have been shared in various forms before, particularly in newspaper columns, during policy debates on national radio and television stations and at academic conferences and have also been the subject of extensive tweets. The use of traditional and social public media to share ideas is driven by the consciousness that many consumers of academic and policy-related content, including elected officials, access these ideas from sources other than books or journal articles, as asserted by Malin and Lubienski (2015). Having created a public appetite for the some of the materials, this book now seeks to expand on those ideas in a more thoroughgoing and comprehensive discourse.

While this book embodies a formal and more rigorous representation of ideas that have been the subject of discussion in social and traditional media, I hasten to declare that it is not necessarily a preferred or superior format, except for academic and policy engagement purposes. One of the fundamental purposes for which writing exists is to share ideas and influence behaviour, and this book fulfils this mandate/purpose. In this regard, I wish to use it as a medium to encourage other writers to broaden the scope of their audiences by engaging social and traditional media to share their ideas.

The wisdom of adopting a variety of media for sharing ideas, and more specifically to take advantage of social and traditional media in sharing academic and policy ideas, has been advanced in a compelling argument by Malin and Lubienski (2015). Malin and Lubienski consider the concern of the extent to which universities are involved in shaping public policy and suggest that one of the most effective ways to influence policy is by using the media. It is this kind of consideration that led me first to engage print and electronic media in the sharing of the ideas contained in this book and, subsequently, to capture them in this form. In this way, they serve as a point of reference, captured in a single document, for convenient access and use by policymakers, practitioners, professionals, revolutionaries and relevant others.

Remler (2016), a professor at the School of Public Affairs of the City University of New York, sought to examine what she described as the often-repeated assertion that 90 per cent of papers published in academic journals never get cited. This presumptive low level of citation is often deemed to equate to low levels of readership. Remler's findings show that the figure was not 90 per cent across the board. She found that only 12 per cent of medicine articles are not cited compared to 82 per cent for the humanities. According to Remler, the non-citation rate for natural science was found to be 27 per cent, while social sciences comes out at 32 per cent. These findings illustrate the profound importance of seeking to share scholarship in diverse forms, and I have sought to achieve this diverse sharing through newspaper articles, as well as via an extensive use of social media. In a way, this book is a kind of summary of a raft of ideas and controversies and several conversations held with several audiences and is being presented here as a dossier to facilitate a more comprehensive source to inform policy action.

The Structure and Focus of the Book

The book is divided into three parts: Issues in Higher Education; Social Activism, Economic Development, Crime; and Leadership and Institutional Development. The overarching message of the book is a call to action. In part 1, I seek to make the case for a new approach to the delivery of higher education, arguing for its centrality in the thrust to pursue economic growth and development in the Caribbean. In the first chapter of part 2 (chapter 3), I examine the role of academics and recommend that this group of citizens needs to be more active in advocating for social change. The discussion advances in chapter 4 and focuses on some of the strategies which governments of the Caribbean should consider in pursuing and measuring economic development. The section concludes with an examination of the problem of crime, which is characterized as a major public health emergency and one of the greatest impediments to sustainable economic growth and development in the Caribbean. The book offers some recommendations on how this social disease may be addressed.

Part 3, covering chapters 6 to 9, explores a select list of leadership and institutional development issues which must be tackled if the objectives of sustainable economic growth and development are to be achieved. In chapter 6, the issue of leadership development as an imperative for the Caribbean is explored with a focus on political leadership. The roles and responsibilities of political leadership in the development of the Caribbean are further examined in chapter 7 through the prism of the relational asset of public trust and its major impediment, corruption.

Having identified the role of political leadership in advancing the development and strengthening of institutions in the Caribbean in chapter 6, and the obligation to deal with the vice of corruption in chapter 7, the focus shifts to the functioning of the public sector in chapter 8 and the role of the public sector in advancing development. The book and the section close with an appeal in chapter 9. The contention made in chapter 9 is that the attainment of the institutional and leadership transformations and advancements (made in the book, generally, and the final section, more specifically) require courageous leadership. The acknowledgement is made that while some of the changes that are necessary to achieve development may be subject to policy, including legislation, courage cannot be legislated or even demanded. Thus, an appeal is made for the exercise of courage.

Issues Facing the Caribbean

This book is written for a Caribbean audience; however, any reader outside the Caribbean will see that it is easily applicable to some other contexts, since it is informed by a focus on issues which affect developing countries and small states, generally but particularly within the Caribbean. While perspectives are diverse with respect to the challenges facing Caribbean countries, there is a broad consensus on the major issues. Calmera and Goede (2015) identify twelve major issues which they contend pose challenges to the Caribbean, among them poverty, crime, good governance and education. Dujon (2013) also lists ten factors which he attributes to being largely responsible for the underdevelopment of the Caribbean. His list includes governance without vision, poor labour planning, a fractured education system and policies that drive away foreign direct investment. Collins (2006) suggests that the major issues facing the Caribbean are free trade, crime and poverty, while Jessen and Rodriguez (1999) highlight the issue of global and regional integration. Itam et al. (2000) add to the lists, identifying structural issues related to the region's public sector and financing and issues of output and productivity.

The convergence of perspectives in the literature on issues facing the Caribbean shows five clear thematic patterns which are the major focus of this book. They are education, globalization, productivity, the public sector, crime and governance. It is my contention that the approaches and resources for dealing with these issues raise questions of leadership, transparency, accountability, social activism and advocacy, and courage. It will require courageous leadership to tackle the issues of crime and lethargy in the public sector, and there will have to be a new era of accountability and transparency if leadership is to be credible and trustworthy. The absence of transparency breeds corruption, and as such, given entrenched corruption, there will have to be a resurgence of social activism and advocacy, especially among academia, if the problems of lack of accountability and public corruption are to be rooted out.

The foregoing analysis forms the justification for the focus of this book. While the discussions and examples are largely focused on Jamaica, the list of top issues facing the Caribbean and demonstrated by reference to the scientific literature proves that all the issues are relevant to the Caribbean and social media, which are similarly informed by events in Jamaica and other Caribbean countries. The focus on Jamaica is arguably further justified because the manifestation of some of these problems in Jamaica are more acute and chronic than in other countries, but the need for urgency in dealing with these problems in all of our Caribbean countries is not diminished by their comparatively less severe manifestations.

Notwithstanding the case made earlier in reliance on the scientific literature concerning the relevance on the issues discussed in this book to Caribbean countries generally, I share three examples – public-sector reform, corruption and crime – which have broad Caribbean application. As it relates to public-sector reform, most Caribbean countries, as former British colonies, operate with a public-sector bureaucracy which was inherited from Britain. Most of these former colonies are struggling with how to adapt their public sectors to meet the demands of the modern era. Thus, the discussion in chapter 8 on public-sector reform is applicable to some degree to the entire Caribbean.

The socio-economic problems of corruption, crime and violence represent another example of a broad application. In the area of corruption, the 2018 ranking of Transparency International shows that of 180 countries and territories ranked, no Caribbean country was in the illustrious top ten or top twenty positions. Only two Caribbean countries, Barbados and Bahamas, placed in the top thirty slots, at twenty-fifth and twenty-ninth, respectively. This means that only two Caribbean countries were ranked as not being very corrupt given that they were positioned in the top thirty. St Vincent and the Grenadines was placed in the forty-first position, while Dominica placed at forty-fifth and St Lucia at fiftieth. Six Caribbean countries placed between fifty and one hundred, including Jamaica in seventieth position and Guyana at ninety-third. This profile suggests that the issue of corruption is a major problem facing

Caribbean countries. Transparency International has argued that one of the greatest obstacles to sustainable economic and social development is corruption. This position is supported by the International Monetary Fund and other international agencies.

In the area of crime, as shown in table 0.1, five Caribbean countries are among the top ten countries in the world with the highest rates of murder per capita according to the 2019 World Population Review report. In the 2017 rankings, Jamaica topped the Caribbean at 57 murders per 100,000 members of the population and was second globally. Despite falling to 47/100,000 in 2019, Jamaica again topped the Caribbean to be fourth globally. Belize remained second in the Caribbean in both 2017 and 2019, holding fourth and sixth positions globally. Six other Caribbean countries made it to the top ten across two ranking periods in 2017 and 2019. These rankings show that the Caribbean faces a major problem with crime, accounting for 50 per cent of the top ten most violent countries in the world, based on murders per capita.

Table 0.1. Murder Rates in Caribbean

Country	# of Murders per 100,000 Population in 2017	Position in Global Top 10
Jamaica	57	2
Belize	37.9	4
Bahamas	29.8	6
St Lucia	29.6	8
Dominica	25.7	10
Country	# of Murders per 100,000 Population in 2019	Position in Global Ranking
Jamaica	47	4
Belize	37.6	6
St Vincent and the Grenadines	36.46	7
St Kitts and Nevis	34.23	8
Trinidad and Tobago	30.88	10

Leadership and Power

One of the themes examined in this book is that of power and its relationship to leadership. The examination of these issues reflects my biases and philosophical understanding of power and its role in effective leadership. My philosophical understanding of power and its relationship to leadership is principally that effective leadership is based on trust, and the level of trust others have in a leader is influenced by the leader's exercise of power.

My interpretation and philosophical construction of trust is informed by Hurley (2006), who defines trust as confident reliance on someone when one is in a position of vulnerability, as well as by Mayer, Davis and Schoorman (1995), who characterize trust as the willingness to be vulnerable to the actions of another. Hurley's position is not unique, but is buttressed by eminent writers on power such as Galbraith (1983), Handy (1993) and de Moll (2010). Central to the collective understandings of these authorities is the view that the responsible exercise of power includes variables such as accountability, responsiveness, transparency and trust. These concepts are explored in detail in various sections of the book.

A motif which cuts across the concepts of accountability, responsiveness, transparency and trust as desired behaviours on the part of the leader is egalitarianism. In this regard, the role of citizens in exercising their power is examined both from the perspective of citizen power via the ballot box and through the exercise of activism carried out by organized professionals. To this end, I explore the issue of social activism, which I regard as a dying quality among Caribbean citizens and especially academics and the professional middle class. While there has been a drastic decline in social activism by academics and the middle classes in Caribbean society, there have been three instances of tremendous activism and determination by two groups of professionals in 2014, 2018 and 2019.

In 2014, members of the academic, administrative and ancillary staff of the University of Technology, Jamaica (UTECH), with the support of their unions, publicly demanded the university answer questions about its management. The university initially resisted, but the employees were relentless in their demands, so eventually it had to respond. The strong advocacy of the staff eventually led to a restructuring at the management level of the institution. There was a repeat of the acts of vigilance by members of the academic staff of UTECH in late 2019 when they protested, demanding equity in treatment compared to other academics in other universities in Jamaica.

Another powerful display of activism which planted a seed of optimism took place in 2018, when the prime minister of Jamaica decided to appoint the chief justice temporarily, effectively on probation. This unusual decision drew consternation and disapproval from several sections of society. Despite this, the prime minister and the members of his government stood firm in their position. In what may be described as an unprecedented move, ninety-seven members of the judiciary took collective action and issued a statement opposing the decision of the government. The statement by members of the judiciary read in part: "Declarations of the prime minister relative to the acting appointment unquestionably have serious implications for the fundamental principles of the separation of powers and the independence of the judiciary. These are principles of great jurisprudential value as they form the foundation of our constitutional democracy and which are critical imperatives for the protection and preservation of the rule of law" (paragraph 5). But even with such strong opposition, the government's position remained unchanged even though its rhetoric softened. This softened rhetoric was reflected in a statement which read in part: "There was never any intention on the part of the Executive to 'supervise or direct' the Judicial branch. The Prime Minister in accordance with the Constitution recommended someone to perform the roles and functions of the Chief Justice. It was not intended to have the recommended person act indefinitely. It was always the intention of the Government in short order to appoint the Chief Justice." Though the government softened its rhetoric, it retained its position, which another group of professionals, the Jamaican Bar Association, found difficult to accept. It was their intervention, by way of a threat to take legal action by taking the matter to the Privy Council, the country's highest court, which resulted in the permanent appointment of the chief justice.

These cases illustrate that an important component of development in the Caribbean is the exercise of power by citizens, who are expected to hold their leaders to account and take actions that are necessary to safeguard the interests of the country. All three cases discussed earlier illustrate the power of people in a democracy and the efficacy of collective action.

There are two principal frames within which the heightened call to public policymakers to be responsive to citizens is to be understood. The first frame is based on the biblical (and natural justice) principle of "to whom more is given of him or her is more demanded" (Luke 12:48, KJV). The second and more critical frame is the fact that public policymakers (that is, holders of elected office) commit to electors/citizens that they would use their time in office to advance the interests of the entire society. By virtue of holding public office, these elected officers have greater means of doing so – more than others who aspire to transform society. However, this does not absolve those of us who do not hold public office from executing one of the primary civic duties which we are called upon to exercise, which is that of holding persons in public office accountable for what they promised.

An important starting point from which persons who hold public office may inform their agenda, and thus effectively determine the summons to action to which they will respond, is by setting out a bold vision for their country. The need for Caribbean leaders to carve out such a vision is as urgent in this, the first half of the twenty-first century, as it was in the second half of the twentieth century, when most countries of the Caribbean achieved internal self-government and later political independence. Several Caribbean founding fathers set the kind of example that the current generation of elected officials needs to emulate. For example, Norman Manley (1893–1969) was one of the Caribbean's early leaders of the internal self-government movement and one of the founding fathers of the Jamaican nation. In carrying out his important and seminal activity in the building of a nation, Manley was clear about what he desired his contribution to be. He led the movement for self-government and independence, served as chief minister from 1955 to 1959 and as premier from 1959 to 1962. He also founded the People's National Party in 1938. Manley interpreted his role, and that of the leaders of his generation, as that of securing political independence for Jamaica. He was satisfied that the important task of economic independence was that of the generation after him, having played a key role in the shaping of the Jamaican constitution.

In somewhat of a similar way, Eric Williams (1911–81) was guided by a vision that defined his role as that of undoing the economic disparities of his island home, Trinidad. The pain of the struggles that his family and others like him experienced in the brutal social and racial hierarchy of British rule fuelled his resolve. While he studied in Britain, he encountered even more severe racism and again sprang into action to assume as one of his chief tasks the need to expose, for the benefit of his fellow regional and national citizens, the hypocrisy and dishonesty of the reasons for the abolition of the slave trade and slavery. His first exploration of this was in his doctoral thesis, "The Economic Aspects of the Abolition of the Slave Trade and West Indian Slavery", which was published in 1944 as *Capitalism and Slavery*. He reiterated and expanded on his arguments in later works, including his classic *From Columbus to Castro: The History of the Caribbean, 1492–1969*. Williams's (1970) basic argument was that it was not humanitarian and moral concerns which gave rise to the abolitionist movement in Europe, but economic and strategic ones. Like Norman Manley, he founded a political party in 1955 – People's National Movement – and later served as prime minister of Trinidad and Tobago from 1956 to 1981.

According to Callaghan (n.d.) Errol Barrow (1920–87), the father of the Barbadian nation and one of the country's ten national heroes, led that country's fight for independence – which it secured in 1966. Like Manley and Williams, Barrow hailed from a family of social activists and politicians who were known for their strong opposition to racism and social stratification, which were characteristics of that small island state. Barrow's early exposure to activism navigated his pursuit to overthrow racism and inequality and informed a wide range of policy measures which he implemented in Barbados. Some of these included national health insurance, social security and free education up to the tertiary level.

The similarities among the architects of Caribbean independence were their bold activism and their willingness to challenge the dominance and control of the Western powers. Each of these leaders laid the foundation for what was to become an era of political ferment and intellectual richness in the policy debates of the late 1960s into the 1970s. By contrast, the period of the late 1990s into the present era has seen what may be described as a docile response to the hegemonic political tendencies of the north and a capitulation to the wishes of the powerful. Not only is political vision and ferment of ideas lacking but so is open intellectual contest of ideas and stridency in defence of those ideas. The period of the 1980s was characterized by a resurgence of colonialism influenced by the policies of Ronald Reagan, president of the United States (1980–88), and Margaret Thatcher, British prime minister (1979–90). Their negative influence on the economic fortunes and politics of the Caribbean are analysed by Manley (1983) and (1987) in *Jamaica: Struggle in the Periphery* and *Up the Down Escalator*.

Having such a precedent set for them by the founding fathers of some of the Caribbean nations, this current set of Caribbean leaders has a frame of reference from which they can craft their vision, if they are to utilize their power successfully. They are therefore obligated to first interpret the demands that the realities of their respective countries (and the region as a whole) place upon them and craft an enabling vision to take such action as is warranted by those demands.

Part 1

Issues in Higher Education

1.

Higher Education in the Caribbean and the Challenge of Global Competition

One of the threats faced by Caribbean countries generally is global competition to its delivery of higher education. This competition is being posed in relation to both quality and cost and therefore introduces the question of the sustainability of higher education in the Caribbean. While the threat is posed to all higher education institutions in the Caribbean, it is most potent with respect to the region's largest and only regional university, the University of the West Indies (UWI). The chief source of the threat is the General Agreement on Trade in Services (GATS), which was signed by Caribbean governments after it came into force in 1995.

The General Agreement on Trade in Services: Structure and History

The GATS is the first multilateral agreement covering trade in services. It was negotiated during the last round of multilateral trade negotiations, called the Uruguay Round, and came into force in 1995. The GATS, a framework of rules governing services trade, establishes a mechanism for countries to make commitments to liberalize trade in services and provides a mechanism for resolving disputes between countries.

The service sector encompasses a wide and disparate array of economic activity, ranging from traditional sectors such as transport, communications, finance, energy and tourism to new and dynamic areas such as software development, environmental and educational services (Sauvé 2002). Trade in services is customarily defined as operating in four modes, the first and chief of which is cross-border. The others are consumption abroad, commercial presence and presence of a natural person. These will be examined in further detail later.

Five years after the GATS was passed, Mattoo (2000, 1) highlighted some of the challenges that developing countries would face and argued that rather than resisting liberalization of domestic markets and seeking dilution of multilateral rules, developing countries "need to push aggressively for liberalization of domestic services markets, emphasizing competition more than a change of ownership". Chanda (2002, 17) also showed sensitivity to this concern, noting "that perhaps the single biggest misapprehension about the GATS is that it will force developing countries to open up all service sectors to foreign competition and compel them to privatize and deregulate services".

The observations of Mattoo and Chanda highlight what has become a major concern some Caribbean countries have about GATS, namely, that in its current form it does not favour higher education institutions in small developing countries, but rather places them at great risk to large universities in developed countries. The ideal solution may appear to be the re-negotiation of GATS, but in the unlikely event of this happening, and having not happened some fifteen years since the signing of the agreement, the question facing regional governments generally, and higher education institutions in particular, is how best to navigate GATS.

GATS is best understood within the context of globalization and internationalization. Altbach and Knight (2007) argue that globalization is the context of economic and academic trends that are part of the reality of the twenty-first century. Dicken (1992) holds a similar view, arguing that globalization is qualitatively different from internationalization. He contends that globalization represents a more advanced and complex form of internationalization. Internationalization, he suggests, implies a degree of functional integration between internationally dispersed economic activities. Al-Rodhan and Stoudmann (2006) suggest that globalization consists of several components. These components include economic integration, policy transfer across borders, knowledge transmission and reproduction of power relations.

A close study of world history will reveal that the globalization project is perhaps the oldest and most enduring cultural-political project in human history. The first real attempt at globalization began with Alexander the Great in the fourth century BCE; he sought to export and infuse Greek civilization to and in other cultures and economies (Hart-Davis 2015). But Sen (2002) is a little less pan-historical, arguing that the globalization project began about five thousand years ago with an attempt at economic, cultural and political unification of the world. Collier and Dollar (2002) trace globalization in the modern era back to the nineteenth century and identify three waves from then to the present. The first wave they suggest covers 1870–1914, which was characterized by economic integration and the flow of labour from densely populated countries to less populated countries. This phase, they suggest, produced, among other things, a level of xenophobia and fear of cultural assimilation that was followed by a retreat into nationalism between 1914 and 1950, which represented a kind of cooling-off period.

The second phase of globalization, according to Collier and Dollar (2002), was 1950–80, which witnessed close integration among the rich countries in Europe and North America, along with Japan. They explain that the North Atlantic Treaty Organization, the Organisation for Economic Co-operation and Development (OECD), and the General Agreement on Trade and Tariffs represent this process of political and economic integration among the rich countries during this phase. One of the manifestations of this phase in the Caribbean was the migration of people from the West Indies to the United Kingdom to meet labour supply demands (which also saw the birth of the Windrush generation).

The third phase of globalization, which began in the early 1980s, is characterized by very rapid technological advancement in transport and communications, a high rate of flow of labour, higher rates of economic growth and, of course, the advent of social media – which is perhaps the most potent tool of cultural integration. Given the insights from the structure and history of the GATS, it comes as no surprise then that the positioning of the higher education system of our region as a force for development and growth and as a vehicle to overcome the social and economic difficulties and deficiencies that have been encountered has been beset by a myriad of problems. Among these have been political misdirection and missteps, global developments over which weak nation-states have had little control and the collective failure to overcome the limiting political shackles of colonialism. However, as we have embarked on the third decade of the twenty-first century, we are faced with challenges and demands of a different but no less daunting nature. The world has become completely borderless in terms of the economic control that is being exerted by powerful countries over less powerful and small developing nation-states. This reality of borderlessness, or deterritorialization, presents some challenges, which though not insurmountable, will have significant implications for higher education.

GATS and Globalization

Tilak (2011) posits that globalization and internationalization have been the dominant themes of policy discussions on higher education in almost all countries of the world since the start of the twenty-first century. He cites a 2008 study, which found that the internationalization of higher education was a concern for 73 per cent of higher education institutions around the world. He notes from this same study that many countries welcomed globalization in the 1990s based on the expectation that it would bring unprecedented prosperity to all; with increased trade and flows of foreign direct investment and skilled labour between countries, many countries have been awakened to the realization that globalization is really designed to maintain the global capitalist system.

Tilak (2011) also asserts that many academics in developing as well as advanced countries are against the trends that have emerged with the internationalization of higher education, which he says have become more worrisome with the advent of the GATS. Tilak relies on Suárez-Orozco and Qin-Hilliard (2004) in defining globalization as a system characterized by a set of processes that are designed to de-territorialize important economic, social and cultural practices from their traditional boundaries in nation-states. Tilak acknowledges that globalization of education and internationalization are different concepts. In the same vein, however, he concedes that they are basically the same thing, as the removal of boundaries means the unification of the world's education system by facilitation of the free flow of students and teachers, through reduction of all the various kinds of barriers that exist. Tilak affirms the perspective of Knight and de Wit (1999), who argue that internationalization and globalization are different in the sense that globalization can be thought of as the catalyst to which internationalization is the response. Internationalization, according to Altbach and Knight (2007, 2), "includes the policies and practices undertaken by academic systems and institutions . . . to cope with the global academic environment".

The consequence of these definitions is threefold. Academic services, specifically higher education, have been caught up inexorably in the globalization wave, and thus the era of unrelenting competition in higher education is the new norm. Furthermore, in the same way economies are integrating in models such as the Trans-Pacific Partnership (from which President Trump withdrew the United States and now desires to return to but may be unable to). Additionally, in order to achieve this integration, higher education institutions will need to carefully examine their policies and practices, to determine the extent to which they are responsive to the needs and realities of a globalized and interconnected world. The foregoing definitions suggest the need for a closer examination of the impact of globalization and its impact on higher education. This examination is most effectively undertaken by an exploration of the concepts of borderlessness and internationalization.

Borderlessness and Its Implications for Higher Education in the Caribbean

An important sociopolitical and culture-economic concept in the analysis of globalization and internationalization is the concept of borderlessness. Kosmützky and Putty (2016) explain that the term borderlessness is used interchangeably with transnational, offshore and cross-border, adding that transnational higher education has grown exponentially as a worldwide phenomenon in recent years. Importantly, they note that all "four terms highlight the distinction between the traditional international mobility of students and academics across borders and new forms of global flows of programs, providers and institutions, and new rationales for mobility" (9). Knight (2014) elaborates on the concept of mobility, arguing that it has moved from people (students, faculty and scholars) to programmes (twinning, franchise and virtual) to provider (branch campus) mobility and, most recently, to the concerted development of education hubs. The interplay of these four concepts conveys both pragmatic and philosophical meanings. According to Kosmützky and Putty (2016, 21), "cross-border is concerned with the *traversing* of existing borders and is tied to global educational trade and is related to policies on provision, regulation, or governance (including quality assurance), thus bringing into relief the national/local dimension".

The implication of borderlessness for higher education is the threat it poses to small and underfunded universities, whose survival will require some form of trade protection. At the same time, the future of all higher education institutions, both large and small, depends upon their capacity to attract customers while competing in a marketplace without borders. Concomitantly, higher education institutions in small, developing states will have to shift their thinking and operational philosophy from aid to trade, according to Coleman (2003). This literally means that universities in given locales will have to assess not so much their competitiveness, but what I would call their "contribution" and collaborative advantage and seek partnerships to leverage those advantages as they seek to grow their markets and their market share. In this regard, the strategic decision of the UWI to plant a presence on every continent is not only visionary but an absolute necessity.

The real impact of borderlessness for the Caribbean can be examined by taking account of the fact that in 2018 there were at least seven major US universities operating in Jamaica in partnership with local colleges or private universities: this is a significant indicator of understanding what borderlessness truly means. Some of these include Central Connecticut, East Connecticut, Temple University, Pennsylvania and Florida International. To deepen this understanding, consider also that there are universities from the United Kingdom and Canada operating in partnership with local entities. Additionally, there are about another ten operating independently of local entities, and among them they are offering over thirty programmes accredited by the University Council of Jamaica (2018) from the bachelor's to the doctoral level.

A similar picture of borderlessness is present in Trinidad and Tobago, with large universities such as University of Bristol, Cambridge, London and

Nottingham, among others, in partnership with colleges and universities. So advanced is the idea of borderlessness that some of these overseas institutions advertise encouraging students from other parts of the world to come to Trinidad and Tobago as though that is their base. This picture is replicated across the Caribbean with overseas universities setting up campuses in several countries, including Antigua, Bahamas, Barbados and Cayman. What this suggests is that there are simply no borders anymore and the world is one large village. However, only those who have the capacity to move across the landscape will have the advantage. Thus, having been deprived of trade protection, universities in the Caribbean will need to find ways to compete with large multinational universities and become international universities themselves (in the case of national universities) and multinational or multiregional universities, in the case of UWI. In the case of UWI, the process towards multiregionality has begun but needs to be intensified.

To set borderlessness in a global context, what we are experiencing in the Caribbean is minor compared to what is taking place in other parts of the world. Faust (2010) calls attention to the expansion of the European Union's study abroad programme, Erasmus, which sends hundreds of thousands of students and faculty to four thousand institutions in thirty-three countries each year. Faust also highlights the astounding development whereby the Persian Gulf states have recruited international branch campuses with investments in the hundreds of millions of dollars. Faust notes that the Education City in Doha involves six American universities on fourteen square kilometres of land. In addition, New York University opened a campus in Abu Dhabi in 2010 and as of 2017 had enrolled students from eighty-eight countries reflecting a diversity of seventy-seven different languages. The number of nationalities of students enrolled on this campus more than doubled in seven years.

Faust also reports that in 2010 when the university opened students from thirty-nine nationalities were enrolled. A similar situation appears across Asia, Faust notes, with some nearly two hundred branch campuses of Western universities in Asia and the Middle East. A 2015 report of the Cross-Border Education Research Team at State University of New York shows that as of that date there were 229 international branch campuses around the world with another 22 in development. The report cites the United States and United Kingdom as the largest "exporters" of international branch campuses, with 50 and 27, respectively, but found that Russia, with 13 campuses in countries such as Belarus, Albania and Azerbaijan, had overtaken Australia's 11 branch campuses. The Cross-Border Education Research Team's 2017 report indicated that these four countries remained the global players in international branch campus operations. What these reports reveal is the widespread practice of transnationalism in higher education, and that reality potentially portends grave challenges for higher education institutions in small developing countries.

Internationalization and Its Implications for Higher Education in the Caribbean

The internationalization of university education is a long-standing practice. Killick (2014) defines internationalization as a strategic response of a university to the globalization of our world. Tilak (2011) notes that the phenomenon is not new but has been central to how universities have operated from medieval times, particularly with the movement of scholars across countries and regions. The driving force behind the modern practice of internationalization, Killick (2014) observes, is the need to generate fees from international students and the securing of an international brand. Haigh (2002) suggests that internationalization is also concerned with preparing students for the global marketplace. The concept is closely related to borderlessness. In modern times, staff and student exchanges have perpetuated the practice of internationalization, both of which were intended to foster academic, social and cultural enrichment and cross-fertilization of ideas, Tilak suggests.

Tilak (2011) provides a helpful discussion on the construct in which he laments that the original purpose of internationalization was primarily focused on cross-cultural enrichment. This primary reason is fading fast, he suggests, and is being replaced by a genre that is based largely, if not exclusively, on economic considerations. According to Tilak (2011, 26), "the new types of internationalization that are booming include the establishment of offshore institutions, campuses, branches, and operational bases; franchising; twinning and selling joint and split degrees/diplomas in education; and training through the Internet. Many more new modes of internationalization are emerging, and they seem to be changing the very nature of higher education."

Since higher education institutions are the essential actors in creating well-balanced and constructive internationalization strategies, they must advocate for policy change at the governmental level if the policies are driving internationalization in directions that might not serve long-term academic purposes. In this regard, the most important and ongoing task for all higher education stakeholders remains the continuous examination and evaluation of the effects of internationalization. It includes examining the impact of a more internationally open programme, classroom and institution on students and effects on the creation of new knowledge influenced by exposure to scholars and researchers from other parts of the world. Furthermore, the internationalization of higher education should not be just a mere paper agreement, as the true essence of such collaborations requires execution in an environment that is favourable to the development of the international process. Assessing the impact that graduates from these institutions will have on the society or community in which they live is also the duty of all higher education stakeholders.

Challenges Facing Higher Education

Separate and apart from GATS, the enterprise of higher education faces challenges, and though these challenges are not confined to countries of the Caribbean, they portend greater dangers for countries of the Caribbean and the region more generally, given the size of our economy, our dependence on extra-regional support and our capacity to withstand shocks to our economy.

Bernal (2019) articulates the scope of the challenges facing higher education institutions in the Caribbean in a crisp and succinct manner, noting that the centuries-old model of granting a four-year degree to students who attend a university at a particular geographic location is outdated. He further argues that the dominance of countries such as the United States and Great Britain in the higher education market is being challenged by China and India and thus implies that in the same way that China and India have succeeded in challenging the dominance of the United Kingdom and the United States, universities in the Caribbean can also become more competitive globally. Bernal states, however, that if universities in the Caribbean are to survive locally (given the access that nationals of the region have to universities outside the region), let alone compete globally, they will have to expand their modes of delivery, especially through online learning.

The challenges facing higher education in the Caribbean are not unique. Allaire (2018) and Rawls (1999), respectively, identify five challenges facing higher education institutions (HEIs) in the United States. Their lists include rising costs, growing privatization of institutions and the need to improve student completion rates and strengthen the management and governance systems. These challenges have direct implications for HEIs operating in small and developing countries in a borderless world. These factors are similar to those faced by Caribbean higher education institutions, as Bernal (2019) indicates.

Vedder (2017) and Pazzanese (2017), from a more global standpoint, offer similar perspectives as those that are more localized. Vedder (2017) provides a list of seven challenges, which includes higher service delivery cost, maintenance costs to traditional brick-and-mortar campuses, competition from entities that are able to offer certification at lower costs and the narrowing of the gap between what persons with degrees are able to earn and those with high school diplomas, given the nature of the knowledge and information and communication technology (ICT)–driven economy. Pazzanese (2017), reporting on a higher education forum of the Economic Club of Washington

DC in 2017, identifies the three top issues emanating from the forum as the key issues affecting higher education; these are excellence, access and affordability.

Looker (2018), writing from the perspective of UK universities, and drawing on the proceedings of a conversation among over one hundred administrators of HEIs, identifies six main issues facing higher education. The reflections of this group of administrators are instructive. While noting the need to align costs to strategic goals, Looker points out that income from international students is a major source of revenues for UK universities, accounting for £23 billion annually in a context of annual costs of a mere £2 billion. While the fear of the UK administrators appears to be their heavy reliance on international income, the fact is that the attractiveness of, and ease of access to, these metropolitan higher education institutions represents one of the challenges facing universities in the Caribbean region (as well as other developing regions) in a borderless world. In essence, it appears that borderlessness is a general cause of fear among countries. In the case of a developed country such as the United Kingdom, the fear is that their dependence on international students might not be sustainable, while for the Caribbean, the fear is that the United Kingdom's higher education lure will render their institutions of higher learning unsustainable. The implications of the foregoing for Caribbean HEIs concern the measures that must be taken to combat the reality of borderlessness and its sanctioning, which is embedded in the GATS.

GATS and Its Impact on the UWI

An analysis of the potential impact of GATS on the UWI will illustrate the extent of the problem posed by this trading agreement. When the reality of the free movement of international universities as sanctioned by GATS dawned on the UWI back in 2004, the council of the university established a task force to determine the status and nature of commitments made by Caribbean governments under GATS. It was decided that the task force would engage the Regional Negotiating Machinery that was set up at the time to research and provide relevant information to help create a better understanding of GATS, and particularly its implications for the higher education sector in the region. Among the concerns of the UWI was the prospect that extra-regional universities would be able to operate freely in the region, thereby placing it under the strain of increased competition by players which were more resourced and globally recognized. The ethos created by GATS was that higher education was a commodity that could be freely traded, and within the context of international trade and in the absence of tariff barriers, it would be the strongest which would survive.

This legitimate fear of what GATS could mean for its survival was based on the view held by the UWI that regional governments had signed onto something about which they were not quite informed. This view was transmitted via the Jamaica Information Service (JIS) on 27 April 2004 in a report which carried the news of the establishment of the task force. The news story stated in part:

> It became evident during the discussions that many Caribbean governments lacked the capacity to carry out the research that was necessary for formulating effective policy responses to the GATS and that commitments might be made without fully appreciating the far-reaching implications for their national education policies. It was also noted that The UWI might be put at a disadvantage in relation to overseas-based institutions, since it was a regional body operating within the context of binding commitments being made by its individual "shareholders" to international agreements which did not recognize such regional entities.

An entire decade later, Frater (2015) appears to reinforce the notion that policymakers had not fully appreciated the impact of GATS on higher education. Frater suggested that Jamaican trade policymakers had suggested that GATS presented opportunities to position the country's higher education sector as an export industry, given its advantage, which included the English language. The policymakers so implicated had referenced Australia and New Zealand in how they had marketed their system to Asian countries. The approach taken by Australia and New Zealand invites consideration by the UWI and other regional universities on how they market their higher education products to other regions of the globe. The UWI from its inception was fashioned on the premises of internationalization. In fact, the UWI, as the University College of the West Indies, was founded as an international university and staffed by an international faculty and attracting international students. Over the seventy years of its existence, the UWI has remained faithful to that original self-understanding of being universal in its operation and disposition. Under its current Triple A strategy (UWI 2017), which targets having a physical presence on all continents and strengthening its online offerings, the UWI is aiming to achieve world ranking as an internationally recognized research university. The UWI's commitment to internationalization is unlike what some universities are pursuing, which may best be described as glocalization, according to Robertson (1992) and Drori, Höllerer and Walgenbach (2014). Glocalization, according to Drori et al. (2014), neither results in worldwide homogeneity nor fully preserves national differences, but rather leads to interlacing convergences and divergences. This phenomenon of glocalization seems to be the defining quality of higher education today, and thus the future survival of universities will rest on the number of countries and continents in which they have a presence, whether physically, virtually or both, as argued by the UWI in its Triple A strategy. The ability to access education markets unimpeded is one of the distinct benefits of the GATS, and the need to ensure that the GATS operates fairly is paramount. While GATS may present some disadvantages to HEIs in small developing economies, it nonetheless provides an opportunity for these HEIs to take advantage of the free movement of trade in services which is guaranteed under the agreement.

If the HEIs in the Caribbean are to withstand the likely adverse consequences of GATS, discussed earlier, there are some key steps that they must take. These steps are necessary for several reasons, chief of which is that the socio-economic transformation of the region depends on a strong and world-class education system. If the forces of globalization result in the decimation of indigenous institutions, their weakening will affect the developmental prospects of the region. This assertion is entrenched in the idea that the path to the sustainable development of any country is through the quality of its education system (Bernal 2019).

Key Actions for Contending with GATS

It is my position that GATS, at least in its current form, was a mistake since it places small developing countries at an economic, social and human resource disadvantage. Given this level of disadvantage, HEIs must now tackle the necessity of building resilience to buffer the potentially damaging effects of the free trade era represented by GATS. There are three critical steps which I submit these institutions must take in order to achieve this. Aspects of these steps may have greater relevance for the UWI, given its size and dependence on funding from regional governments, but many of the considerations are relevant to all HEIs across the Caribbean as well as private institutions which are owned locally. The three steps are:

1. Carefully analysing the major challenges and obstacles facing HEIs;
2. Identifying opportunities and approaches to higher education management, taking account of the realities of free trade; and
3. Developing strategies for grasping the opportunities and overcoming the obstacles.
   a. The first and most fundamental step universities should take to build resilience for combatting the impact of GATS is to undertake a careful analysis of the major challenges and obstacles facing HEIs.
   b. Having isolated these challenges and obstacles, universities must now utilize these to identify opportunities and approaches to higher education management within the context of the realities of free trade.

c. After universities have identified these specific challenges, and collating those most relevant to building resilience, they will now move to develop strategies targeted at grasping the opportunities and overcoming the obstacles.

The three foregoing steps are aligned to the categories of movement which Altbach and Knight (2007) and Tilak (2011) identify as features of GATS, namely:

1. *Consumption abroad.* The consumer moves to the country of the provider. This mode includes traditional student mobility.
2. *Commercial presence.* The service provider establishes facilities in another country, including branch campuses and joint ventures with local institutions.
3. *Presence of natural persons.* This mode includes persons, including professors and researchers, who temporarily travel to another country to provide educational services.

Estimates of international student recruitment show that there has been exponential growth in the numbers since the turn of the century, quadrupling to reach five million between 1990 and 2014, according to Global Engagement and Research at StudyPortals. This same source also estimates that by 2025, this number is projected to reach eight million. One of the UWI's strategic imperatives must be to ensure that it increases its current share of this market exponentially. These estimates suggest that the market for international students is huge and as such, universities which price and promote their products competitively can command a substantial share of the higher education market (Bernal 2019).

While GATS and its driving force – globalization – as well as its consequential development – internationalization – pose clear risks to the survival of indigenous universities, collectively, these phenomena also present opportunities which, if approached creatively, could result in growth and expansion of HEIs in the Caribbean. I wish to propose what I call an alphabet model that will result in the growth and expansion of higher education. This model covers constructs related to the first five letters of the alphabet with a double use of E, thus ABCDE[2]. This model explores a growth and expansion strategy for higher education.

Adopt a More Inclusive Approach to Strategic Planning

The first element of this model calls for HEIs to adopt new approaches to strategic planning. HEIs, particularly those which benefited from government funding, did not need to engage in extensive strategic planning to remain viable.

This situation changed since the 2007–8 global economic recession. Since then, many HEIs have been struggling financially as governments in the jurisdictions in which they operate have not been able to meet their financial commitments (Hecht 2013). This has been the case with HEIs across the globe, including the regional university of the Caribbean, the UWI and local universities and other tertiary institutions (Thompson 2017). Because of the deep cuts to financing which these HEIs have experienced, many have had to review their approaches to strategic planning. At the UWI, for example, the process of strategic planning was confined only to staff at the very senior levels. One possible explanation for this could be that many staff members would not have had formal exposure to the process of strategic planning; thus, their involvement would not be considered paramount. However, with less financial input from government to finance their operation, HEIs face an increased need to find alternative ways of surviving. One available option is now to design strategic planning approaches that will meaningfully include all members of their staff in the strategic planning process and not only those at the senior management levels.

To maximize the value of this strategy, the university needs to take account of the fact that most faculty members are not familiar with strategic planning as a process. Consequently, the university would have to build the skills and competencies for successful strategic planning by giving these employees some minimum formal exposure to the issues involved in strategic planning.

The issue of inclusivity in strategic planning is reinforced by Litman (2013), who includes among the key principles of effective strategic planning inclusivity and transparency.

Build Inter-institutional Partnerships

In addition to adopting a more inclusive approach to strategic planning, HEIs (confronted with the realities of borderlessness and internationalization in an era in which higher education is a tradeable service) will have to abandon the notion that they can operate independently and with absolute internal autonomy. Instead, they must become willing to enter into inter-institutional collaborations and the building of partnerships. Hecht (2013) notes that the survival of universities in the post-2008 recession-hit global economy depended on the degree to which they could successfully collaborate and, in fact, make collaboration the new competition.

Hecht cited two examples. First, the case of the city of Cleveland, Ohio, in which long-time rival universities and hospitals came together to harness their collective billions to buy, hire and research in order to re-shape the economic future. In the second example, Hecht describes how leaders of ten counties in the areas of Atlanta which had been hardest hit by the economic downturn abandoned their pride, came together and rallied the business community to promote a historic eight billion bond issuance and regional tax increase to address a range of social problems. Jones and Clulow (2012) cite the collaboration between Pfizer and the University of California, which has succeeded in combining the best academic thinking with the drug development expertise of industry, resulting in improvements in the quality of healthcare. A similar collaboration agreement was done between GlaxoSmithKline and the University of Cambridge.

Thus, the future of large and small universities, particularly in developing countries, depends on the extent to which they are willing to collaborate. Pratt et al. (2011) concur with Hecht (2013) on the need for collaboration in a post-recession era. In reflecting on the impact of the global recession, which left many governments in increased debt, Pratt et al. (2011) note that even though political administrations of all stripes recognize the importance of higher education in pulling countries out of economic setback, they made cuts to HEIs. These cuts affected teaching universities as much as they have research universities. It is in light of the severe cuts faced by HEIs, on top of the already exacting challenges from the GATS, that inter-institutional partnerships have become even more critical.

Given the necessity of building partnerships as a strategy of survival, one implication of this for Jamaica, for example, relates to how the government will fund multiple universities given the apparent desire of several teachers' colleges to become universities. One policy question which must be resolved is whether there should be free-for-all, wherein each institution decides on its own future with respect to becoming a university, or whether there should be some policy directive that provides some parameters within which each should operate, informed by some structure of collaboration. I am in favour of an approach which stipulates collaboration with the view to maximizing the use of resources and reducing duplication of services as far as is possible, based on demand.

Pratt et al. (2011) suggest that collaboration between the university and the community represents another area of sustainability for the university. Jones and Clulow (2012) caution that one of the preconditions for collaboration among and between universities will be their willingness to build trust on the issue of intellectual property.

Combine High-Quality Assurance Standards with Faster Decision-Making

Quality assurance in higher education is one of the most vital mechanisms of product quality and consistency. For this reason, HEIs must establish rigorous internal quality assurance measures, as well as submit their entire operations to external quality evaluation. One of the controversial issues that is raised when quality assurance is being debated is the relationship between rigour and efficiency, and specifically whether quality can be assured in quick time. This issue of combining high-quality assurance standards with speed and efficiency is relevant to course, programme and intra- and inter-institutional development activities, on the one hand, and delivery and operation, on the other.

Notwithstanding the value of inter-institutional cooperation both with national and regional jurisdictions and across jurisdictions, HEIs must address competition within their target markets. Given this reality, timely and swift responses to demands for new products and services must be paramount considerations for the leadership of institutions. Late or slow responses could mean losing out on market opportunities or an inability to compete effectively in markets in which other institutions have moved to establish brands that have been adopted in the marketplace.

The UWI has an exceedingly rigorous and lengthy quality assurance process for the approval of new courses, programmes and other developmental initiatives. It is not unusual for a new programme or developmental initiative to take in excess of three years to be approved once the review process begins; this time period does not include the concept development process, which may take several weeks, a couple of months or even a year. Given the freedom permitted under the GATS for HEIs from outside the Caribbean to operate within the region, whether through establishing physical branch campuses or offering programmes online, the risk of long delays in bringing new programmes to the marketplace could mean that potentially attractive programmes being contemplated by the UWI are eclipsed in their market entry by programmes and courses being offered by other universities. In this regard I speak as a programme and course developer within the UWI and have lived through the experiences of waiting years to obtain approval for programmes which the data suggested were in demand in the marketplace.

The call for greater efficiency in the approval process is not to be confused with a presumed call for the relaxing of quality assurance requirements, but is rather based on the recognition that management systems in higher education need to take greater account of the reforms and approaches to business processes in other industries. Kenny (2008) addresses this issue of the need for HEIs to critically examine their processes and to adopt the learning principles of what Senge (1990) calls the learning organization.

Diversify Products and Delivery Pathways

Successful business enterprises owe a large part of their success to being able to offer a wide range of choices to customers. The logic for this is simple. Even among relatively homogenous market segments, there are nuances in the tastes and needs of customers. As such, the ability of an enterprise to attract and retain sizeable market share will depend on how well the enterprise caters to the sub-categories of a given market segment. Against this background, the conception of higher education products must take account of the increasingly diverse market for higher education. While this may mean abandoning some programmes and courses, as well as restructuring delivery, the imperative to diversify is more about adding new product offerings. In practice, what this means is that in addition to traditional degree programmes, HEIs need to become more creative in offering non-degree, competency-based, market-driven, consumer-sensitive options by way of short courses, multimodal delivery options and customized completion pathways.

One of the areas of tremendous opportunity for business expansion for HEIs is international students of both immediate post-secondary (vocational) and early tertiary (undergraduate) students, particularly from developing regions of the world. The rate of growth in these regions has outstripped industrialized countries. Symonds (2017) drawing on a report from the Research Base organization, a consultancy firm in the United Kingdom, notes that student numbers are increasing in Latin America and the Caribbean, East Asia and the Pacific, sub-Saharan Africa and South and West Asia more quickly in the developing world than any place else. According to Research Base, enrolments in academic courses is rising fastest in Africa, with growth there averaging 16 per cent a year. In South and West Asia, the growth is even greater, at 41 per cent a year, but this growth is taking place in vocational courses.

The foregoing twin developments suggest two things. In the first place, the demand for academic courses, as is the case in Africa, is good news for the world. With Africa being the most populous continent, the market for the products of universities globally has suddenly, as it were, expanded. Equally exciting, however, is the strong growth in vocational studies, as is happening in Asia. This development signals that the UWI needs to, if it wishes to take advantage of potential business opportunities in this area, examine ways in which it can work more closely with community colleges to develop and deliver vocational programmes. The previous recommendation concerning pursuing collaboration is relevant in this regard.

Growth in demand for higher education in the Caribbean and Latin America has been robust over the last decade, according to a 2017 World Bank report. The report showed that in the region, the percentage of individuals between the ages of eighteen and twenty-four who are enrolled in higher education rose from 21 per cent in the year 2000 to 40 per cent in 2010. The report notes that while issues of unequal access remain a problem, significant progress has been made, particularly among low- and middle-income groups. The report established that while on average, the poorest 50 per cent of the population represented only 16 per cent of higher education students in 2000, this increased by over half to about 25 per cent in 2013. These developments represent good news for universities in general, and the UWI, in particular.

Given the growth in the international student market in which consumers are seeking both immediate post-secondary and early tertiary training opportunities, some HEIs have adopted what is known as the unbounded university model, one which local and regional universities can adopt. The primary expression of this model is seen in alliances between established and sought-after Ivy League universities and (in the case of the United States) historical black colleges (Pratt et al. 2011). Broadly, these alliances involve the leveraging of market intelligence (research), product demand and market share to boost customer base in offering a wider variety of study and skill-acquisition options.

The global international student population grew from 2.1 million in 2001 to 4.6 million in 2017, a 120 per cent increase. Interestingly, China, which was not named in the top eight in 2001, catapulted to third place behind the United States and United Kingdom in 2017, while Canada and Russia landed at sixth and seventh places, respectively, in 2017 after not being in the top eight in 2011, according to a May 2018 report of Study International. In the Caribbean and Latin America, the growth in HEIs has been rapid in the first decade and a half of the twenty-first century. This has been spurred by significant inputs from the private sector. The result is that the percentage of private HEIs has grown from 43 to 50 per cent between the early 2000s and 2013, according to a 2017 World Bank report. The expectation that growth in the number of HEIs operating in the Caribbean and Latin American region being likely to continue means that the game will be for the survival of the most agile and accessible and those whose products are most aligned to the needs of consumers. This dynamic calls for greater focus by regional universities on the marketing of their products and programmes.

Another element of the unbounded university model is the optimization of advanced technological solutions which allow for the flipping of the classroom, virtual classrooms, online learning and collaborative learning (Nicholas 2008; Sickler 2009). The flipped classroom is one in which students learn at their own pace and time. These classrooms are supported by pre-recorded lectures, podcasts and other forms of prepared materials which students will access at times most convenient to them. The virtual classroom is the facility which allows students to be part of a class without leaving the comfort of their home, and online learning allows students to take a class without ever having to meet the lecturer. These are all useful modalities which HEIs will need to explore as they seek to diversify programmes and pathways. It would not be surprising that a needs analysis could show that these modalities are aligned to many groups of potential students.

It is estimated that by the year 2025 millennials will comprise the majority of the world's population. This has major implications for how HEIs structure their operations, given what has emerged as the preferred study habits of millennials. Millennials engage digitally (texting, tweeting, videos and other means). The immediate relevance of this is that the provision of learning opportunities for this segment of the population must nearly exclusively rely on online and digital means. This further suggests that the creation of physical space is no longer a priority on limited financial resources. McKeachie (2002), Oblinger (2003) and Prensky (2001) found that millennials prefer learning approaches which utilize digital technologies. But the comfort of millennials with digital learning styles is not their only learning characteristic. Millennials are also keen on teamwork and collaboration, as Nicholas (2008) has found. This means that, among other things, in using digitized methods of teaching and learning, universities need not fear that students will become isolated and insular, as the said digital means can be used to build large online human communities. Communities cater to the most basic requirements of what it means to be human, and happily digital technologies do not inevitably undermine the attainment of this important goal. What this means for the delivery of higher education is that rather than investing in buildings as a primary mode of creating space to accommodate growth in the institution's customer base, the investment should be in the natural home for millennials and Generation Z. This means that the major infrastructural resources of the modern university, like satellites, internet, bandwidth and other elements of a digital age, should be emphasized and be made integral to how the institutions are defined.

Embrace the Competition

Based on the assessments of the impact of the GATS, the prognosis is that the international competition for students will intensify, with obvious implications for the Caribbean in which several overseas universities currently operate. Many of Asia's leading countries, including China, Japan, Singapore and Taiwan, and countries in Europe and North America, as well as Australia, have set targets that would see massive increases in their international student populations over approximately ten to fifteen years, ending in 2020 and up to 2025. In some instances, the targets were up to 1,000 per cent. The results show that Germany reached its 2020 target of 350,000 students by the 2016–17 school year. Canada had set a target to attract 450,000 international students by 2022 but was close to that target in 2016 (Geffert 2018). The major global players in international higher education mentioned earlier – Australia, Canada, China, Russia and the United Kingdom – are all committed to market dominance, and this means aggressive competition. Prior to GATS, the competitors of the UWI were local and regional institutions. Post-GATS and for the foreseeable future, the competitors are everywhere. If the UWI and other indigenous HEIs in the Caribbean intend to compete and survive and thrive, regional governments will have to adopt a new mindset which will allow them to invest more heavily in such institutions. Countries such as China, India, Indonesia, Japan, Pakistan and Singapore which are faring well or better economically have seen their governments investing heavily in higher education. The Caribbean cannot see substantial and sustainable improvements in its economies without a corresponding massive investment in higher education. In short, indigenous universities will have to be willing to critique and re-imagine their product development processes and take radical steps to ensure product relevance and responsiveness to market demands, as well as speed in the rollout of said products.

An examination of the performance of the UWI in relation to enrolment shows that for the period 2017–22 it contemplates a 50 per cent increase in enrolment from 49,000 in 2017 to 65,000 in 2022. This is an ambitious target, but the current trend of the data is not encouraging. If the expected growth in student enrolment is to reflect a global presence, both the overall direction of local enrolment and international student enrolment must be reversed. As can be seen in figure 1.1, growth in international student registration has been contracting over the last five years. In 2012–13, with a student enrolment of 50,182, international students accounted for 1,070, or 2.1 per cent. In 2013–14 total enrolment fell marginally by less than 1 per cent but international student enrolment fell by 24 per cent to 805. Thus, while the UWI has an ambitious plan of increasing enrolment by 50 per cent by 2022 compared to its position in 2017, its performance shows that it has seen a significant decline in its international student enrolment, the very area in which it needs to expand in order to remain globally competitive.

Year	2012/2013	2013/2014	2014/2015	2015/2016	2016/2017
Total Enrolment	50,182	50,146	47,395	47,504	47,591
Off which : International	1,070	805	733	783	712
% International	2.1%	1.6%	1.5%	1.6%	1.5%

Figure 1.1. International students as a percentage of the total student population – the UWI (UWI 2018)

As efforts to drive international student enrolment are made, a major factor that must be considered is how global markets and priorities dictated by powerful countries, as well as non-tariff barriers imposed by them, can stifle growth and expansion. Thus, it is not unlikely that while UK and US universities will seek to set up campuses in the Caribbean (and other developing countries), the reverse will not be easy, and branding and history will place the Caribbean at a significant disadvantage.

Engage Entrepreneurship

The notion of engaging entrepreneurship means that if universities are to survive and compete in the twenty-first century, they must become what the European Union has described as entrepreneurial universities (Florea and Florea 2013).

The notion of the "entrepreneurial university" appears to be a relatively new construct which has its genesis in the post-2008 global recession. As mentioned in an earlier segment in this chapter, the recession so significantly altered the financial situations of universities that it became necessary for universities to find alternative income streams. The European Union began to develop a guiding framework for this initiative in March 2011. According to the OECD's Guiding Framework for Entrepreneurial Universities:

> The Guiding Framework began as an idea first discussed at the March 2011 University Business Forum; a European Forum which brings together universities and businesses to look at mechanisms for cooperation and encourage the transfer and sharing of knowledge. A group of participants at the event formulated a recommendation to take a closer look at the underlying concepts and characteristics of an Entrepreneurial University and to come up with a Guiding Framework that would be available to universities as a concrete tool for learning and inspiration. (EC-OECD 2012, 1)

The guiding framework consists of seven elements which are designed to enable a university to assess itself to determine how entrepreneurial it is and then to devise strategies for transforming itself into being more entrepreneurial. The seven elements are:

- Leadership and governance
- Organizational capacity, people and incentives
- Entrepreneurship development in teaching and learning
- Pathways for entrepreneurs
- University–business/external relationships for knowledge exchange
- The entrepreneurial university as an internationalized institution
- Measuring the impact of the entrepreneurial university

The expectation is that by implementing this framework, universities will receive ideas and inspiration that will raise the levels of financial, leadership, governance and organizational capacity of their institutions and thus increase their viability, impact and influence. This undertaking represents an urgent one if HEIs in the Caribbean are to survive and thrive. The fact that universities in developed countries have found it necessary to undertake the measures described signals the urgency of the need for HEIs in developing countries to initiate similar steps.

2.

Financing Higher Education

The ubiquitous question about the funding of tertiary education revolves around the question of "who pays?" The issue has been the subject of extensive, and sometimes complex, discussions, with little definitive resolution. This chapter proposes to offer what I hope will be a simplified approach to financing tertiary education by addressing some issues and laying out some practical guidelines for addressing them. The issue of how Caribbean countries fund tertiary education is genetically connected to the countries' prospects for development and with the threats which face the viability of tertiary education in the Caribbean, as outlined in chapter 1. The issue of how much and how countries in the Caribbean invest in tertiary education, then, becomes an existential question.

Several Caribbean writers and scholars have sought to address this issue. Lewis (2018) proposes a four-point funding model, including requiring universities to demonstrate greater capability in entrepreneurship and supporting developmental needs of countries, listing of universities on the Stock Exchange and universities issuing bonds. In making the case for bonds, Lewis cited the case of the University of Southampton, which offered a forty-year bond and raised £300 million after it was listed in 2017, and is among a small league of listed universities. The Caribbean Policy Research Institute (CaPRI 2009) advances the economic and social arguments to support its basic position that governments of the region should invest more in tertiary education. CaPRI advances that the funding policy of the Jamaican education sector represents a direct subsidy to developed countries, as many graduates faced with massive debt seek employment in other countries, thereby deploying their skills in those countries, and the Jamaican system of funding tertiary education results in those who have more resources benefiting from more state resources, while those with limited access are placed at an even greater disadvantage. CaPRI also suggests that given the challenge with financial resources that Jamaica faces, the solution for the funding of tertiary education does not reside in finding new cash sources, but rather through re-allocation. With respect to its economic argument, the institute recommends that governments see universities not merely as producing graduates, but they should also engage in research which is designed to inform strategies for increasing production, productivity and market opportunities and in the process increase tax revenues. Additionally, on the social side of its argument, CaPRI posits that a funding model that ends up excluding large segments of the population is ultimately counterproductive and undermines the prospects for sustainable development.

There is an important point of convergence between Lewis's position on the place of research and the augmenting of the entrepreneurial inclination of universities and that of CaPRI's economic argument. These positions are relevant to countries in the Caribbean. The key lesson is that tertiary education is a long-term investment. Santiago et al. (2008) argue that an important element of financing tertiary education is in recognizing the important principle of using public funds efficiently and creating a coherent tertiary education system. Such a coherent system of tertiary education means, among other things, Santiago et al. suggest, developing a funding strategy which facilitates the contribution of the tertiary education system to the society and the economy. This process involves designing a funding approach to meet the policy goals sought for tertiary education. These policy goals will inescapably address issues such as quality, cost-effectiveness, equity and institutional capacity.

Kumari and Sharma (2017) describe how India has structured its higher education system to ensure synergy and to create the link between the university and the economy. Under the Indian higher education system, there are three tiers. In tier 1 are the research universities whose focus was on, among other things, studying new global and national economic developments and offering recommendations on how to position the education system to respond. Tier 2 consists of teachers' colleges which, with the support of research outputs from the universities, strengthened and repositioned the processes of preparing teachers for services at the early childhood to secondary levels. In tier 3 are the polytechnics and community colleges whose focus is to prepare skilled and certified workers for all sectors of a highly technologically driven service economy. The programmes of training offered are informed by university-led research. Caribbean governments are urged to adopt the Indian model of linking tertiary education to the direction and requirements of the economy. This practice has been credited with the growth and development India has been experiencing over the last two decades (Kumari and Sharma 2017).

Faust (2010) notes that in India, the numbers attending universities doubled in the 1990s, and demand continues to surge. Faust also highlights the plan by the Government of India to establish eight hundred new institutions of higher education by 2020 in order to more than double the higher education age participation rate from 12.4 per cent to 30 per cent. Although not all Caribbean countries have a fully developed tertiary system, each country can nonetheless create a model for both the funding of access of its citizens to tertiary education and to create a model for how they will engage research outputs from universities engaged in research to support both the elements of a tertiary education system, which they possess, as well as to support their economies.

In addition to a creative funding model for universities to which Lewis (2018) calls attention, the philosophical and policy-oriented approach articulated by CaPRI (2009) and the three-tier Indian model advanced by Kumari and Sharma (2017), there is what I would describe as the industry-alignment Chinese model, which Wu (2006) discusses, and the New Zealand "think tertiary early" approach, which McLaughlin (2003) explains. All these models deserve the attention of Caribbean governments, and each is discussed next.

Industry-Aligned Chinese Model

According to the 2016 Asian Productivity Organization Databook, approximately 50 per cent of the Chinese workforce has been trained in technical and vocational education. This achievement is largely responsible for China's emergence as the new global giant. China had a gross enrolment ratio in tertiary education of 4.46 per cent in 1995 but has seen that grow to over 40 per cent at present with an average annual rate of 12.48 per cent. Part of the explanation for this, and part of the reason China now dominates world exports and is a major funder and implementer of infrastructure projects, is China's emphasis on technical and vocational education training. According to Wu (2006) the 2016 Asian Productivity Organization Databook shows that there are over 2,560 HEIs in China, up from a mere 205 just under seventy years ago. A key fact is that over 1,340 of China's HEIs are technical and vocational education training. The existence of technical and vocational education training institutions is the explanation for China's global dominance in telecommunications, infrastructure, widescale manufacturing and electronics, among others.

Wan-hua Ma (2003), in an article entitled "Economic Reform and Higher Education in China", traces the parallel developments of the Chinese economy and tertiary education system. Ma notes that 1976 marked a turning point in China's political, economic and higher education philosophies. Wan-hua Ma observes that with respect to its political and economic philosophies, China shifted focus from privatization of enterprises to the creation of new enterprises and from promoting property rights to promoting market competition. In relation to its higher education philosophy, the developments were phenomenal.

In 1976, there were 392 HEIs; in 1985, the total number grew to 1,010. In addition, a number of existing colleges and universities were upgraded. According to Ma, in 1977 there was only one institute in economics and finance; in 1987 there were seventy-four. In the areas of politics and law, the number of HEIs moved from one in 1977 to twenty-five by 1987. The number of HEIs in China has increased by over six and a half times in the forty-year period between 1976 and 2016, from 392 in 1976 to a whopping 2,596 as of 2016. Faust (2010) describes the performance of China in relation to the creation of HEIs as the most dramatic higher education explosion in human history. He also notes that between 1999 and 2005, the number of degree earners quadrupled to more than three million. The result of China's development strategy using higher education has resulted in that country producing the world's largest number of PhD scientists and engineers.

With that phenomenal level of expansion in its education system, Ma cites many examples of the impact on Chinese society and economy. He notes, for example, that China has been able not only to solve its local food shortage but attain the status of feeding 22 per cent of the world's population with less than 7 per cent of the world's farm lands. Ma notes further that some ten years after the reform of its higher education system in 1976, annual gross domestic product (GDP) growth in China was 11.8 per cent in 1988; in 1993 the annual growth rate peaked at 13.4 per cent but fell sharply to 9.0 per cent in 1997 and fell further to 7.8 per cent in 2002. In the quarter of a century between 1977 and 2002, China has experienced annual average GDP growth of 9.4 per cent. Though its growth has slowed considerably since, falling by about 50 per cent, China continues to be the fastest-growing economy, with its 2017 rate of growth being 6.8 per cent and projected to be 6.4 per cent in 2018.

Mi Zhou and Louis Vaccaro (2007), in a paper entitled "Strengthening the Relationship between Higher Education and Regional Economic Development", point to the correlation between education and economic development. They note that the essence of the relationship between the Chinese economy and its education system is that the latter prepares research personnel, business leaders and entrepreneurs; provides small business support; invents cutting-edge technologies and business development innovations; develops new products and services; and provides investment assistance. Therefore, the key strategy of China's growth in the number and variety of tertiary educational institutions is deliberate and purposeful alignment between the funding of education and the forecast of global product and service demand. As the Caribbean seeks to grow its tertiary enrolment, there must be a clear alignment between programmes offered and the projected needs of the global market.

The issue of purposeful alignment requires that the government and the universities, as well as the private sector, target funding and programme development to areas of greatest future needs. What the philosophy and policy of alignment means in practical terms is that scholarships, grants and bursaries should be aligned with emerging market and national needs. Some of this is happening, but much more needs to be done. Let us take an example. The World Health Organization recommends that the dentist-to-patient ratio of a country be 1:2,500. The current ratio in Jamaica is 1:17,000. To get Jamaica's ratio to the recommended level by 2030 requires an output of approximately one hundred dentists each year over the next ten years. Both the UWI and UTECH have dentistry programmes, but there is no strategic plan of the government which sets out a roadmap for the training of dentists (and I speak about this matter from the perspective of having worked in a position in which I advised the Government of Jamaica on the provision of scholarships for the training of dentists). By contrast with deficits in the number of dentists is the oversupply of lawyers. The concern about the oversupply of lawyers has been a source of much debate in Jamaica (Vasciannie 2017)

While both the UWI and UTECH law programmes are largely self-financed and thus do not call on state resources commensurate with the size of the cohorts, does that fact preclude the intervention of the government in at least seeking to influence, even if not to dictate, priorities and the re-directing of resources? I think not. It is in fact my position that while the UWI is the regional university and therefore does not fall under the control of any one government, and while UTECH as a university ought to be given some level of autonomy and independence, the imperatives of strategic regional and national development require consultation and collaboration in deciding on how to invest limited resources.

Approaches to Funding Higher Education

New Zealand's model for supporting higher education has received global attention (McLaughlin 2003). Under this model, participation in higher education increased significantly between the 1980s and the present, with McLaughlin (2003) reporting an increase between the 1980s and 1990s.

According to McLaughlin (2003), the number of students in tertiary education in New Zealand increased from 120,000 in the mid-1980s to 282,000 students in 2001. She further notes that the proportion enrolled increased from 20.5 per cent in 1990 to 34.8 per cent in 2001.

The 2014–19 Tertiary Education Strategy of New Zealand (2014) shows that current tertiary participation rates among fifteen- to nineteen-year-olds is

81 per cent, 29 per cent of twenty- to twenty-nine-year-olds, 11 per cent of thirty- to thirty-nine-year-olds and 4 per cent of those aged forty. The strategy document further shows that approximately 50 per cent of New Zealanders aged fifteen and over have a tertiary qualification and 17 per cent have a bachelor's degree or higher.

According to McLaughlin (2003), the factors chiefly responsible for these improvements are (1) the move to central steering of funding of programmes tied to national needs; (2) public/private cost sharing in tertiary education; (3) closing of the opportunity gap in tertiary participation for at-risk groups; (4) moving from funding a smaller number of students at a higher rate to funding a larger number of students at a lower rate; and (5) use of data and research to inform decisions.

I submit that this model is one that Caribbean countries should adopt. Akin to these policy measures was a social strategy called "Think Tertiary Early". Under this strategy families were encouraged to begin planning for tertiary education for their children from birth. There are two simple and critical advantages to this model. First, it enables families to begin preparing for the cost of tertiary education at an early stage, thus there is a longer investment period for the funds they are saving. In the second place, with the contribution of the state, via matching funds, the investment pool becomes larger, and again with the eighteen to twenty years to maturity for each tranche of funds, the growth in the portfolios can be considerable. As appealing as this model appears to be, it is not without its challenges.

The New Zealand model of "Think Tertiary Early" was developed to address two major societal hurdles: the belief that the financing of tertiary was the responsibility of the state and the social perception that debt was a bad thing. With such a mindset, a policy which sought to shift the burden for tertiary education to the family would be resisted. The result is that today the gross tertiary enrolment rate in New Zealand has more than doubled. Two additional features of the New Zealand approach to making tertiary education more accessible and more affordable is the provision of interest-free loans to students who qualify and the linking of repayment obligations and amounts to income. These features represent creative and practical ways for governments in the Caribbean to increase the number of students who acquire tertiary education.

Another approach to funding tertiary education is through what is known as the Child Trust Fund. One model of the Child Trust Fund exists in the United Kingdom and was launched in 2005, but the scheme was discontinued after 2011. Under the operations of the trust, an account with 250 pounds was opened in the name of each child born after a designated date, and the child would access this fund at age eighteen. The child's parents would be able to add to the account but would not be able to withdraw. The funds yielded at age eighteen could be used to finance higher education.

The application of that model for Jamaica has been proposed by Waite (2008) in a presentation made to the Jamaican Parliament. The basic frame of the model is that the government would set aside a specific sum each year on a per capita basis for each child born the previous year, and the parents of each child would make annual payments for eighteen years, at the end of which time the child would have a fund in excess of a million Jamaican dollars towards post-secondary education and training.

An examination of the viability of this proposed policy validates its effectiveness. As of 2020, the average annual number of births in Jamaica over the previous ten years is less than forty thousand, so if that number were used as a benchmark and the government sets aside J$10,000 for each child, the commitment of the government would be J$400,000,000. Four hundred million, in the 2019–20 fiscal year, represents less than one-half of one-tenth of 1 per cent of the country's J$803 billion budget. Such an expenditure would be infinitely easy for the country to afford.

With the government setting aside this J$400,000,000 at the rate of J$10,000 per child, if each parent were encouraged to save J$100 per day or J$3,000 per month for a total of J$36,000 per year for eighteen years, and if those funds attract a tax-free interest rate of 6 per cent, the fund would yield approximately J$44 billion, or an average of J$1.1 million per child. This sum would go a far way to covering tuition for tertiary education.

Gordon (2019) advances the view that the cost of tertiary education should be borne by the student and his or her parents. Part of the reason advanced by Gordon for placing the responsibility on parents and students is the fact that the benefits of a tertiary education accrue to the student and his or her family. According to Gordon, the increased earnings and improved life chances of the tertiary graduate are, for the most part, a personal and private good, as opposed to a public good. It therefore makes sense that individuals foot the bill for their tertiary education. The reality that many Jamaican parents are unable to find the needed funds, in some cases even for food, even after tuition has been paid, invites action on how the financing of the Students' Loan Bureau is to be done. Gordon's position is somewhat at odds with that of CaPRI (2009) in which the latter emphasizes the national development value of tertiary education. The CaPRI approach which considers the disadvantage to families that are unable to afford tertiary education is also at odds with what may be described as Gordon's market model.

Both the socio-economic model of CaPRI and the market model of Gordon have their place, and both should be pursued in a balanced manner, taking account of the need to ensure that the neediest students and families are given state assistance, that universities receive funding for research and that research output and other resources are aligned with developmental needs. In this regard, the following policy positions are worthy of consideration:

1. There should be more focused research by the universities which will lean towards informing and supporting production and productivity pursuits.
2. Repositioning teachers' colleges so that their faculty are more capable of training teachers to facilitate students' creativity (which is the heart of innovation).
3. Expansion, and more strategic deployment, of community colleges in training young graduates in key skills areas to serve the developmental needs of a diverse global, service-driven economy.

While university enrolment and graduation rates have increased dramatically in Jamaica over the last forty years, enrolment rates in the countries with UWI campuses have seen a decline. At the St Augustine Campus in Trinidad and Tobago, enrolment fell steadily from approximately 19,500 in the 2013–14 year to about 18,000 in the 2016–17 year. At the Cave Hill Campus in Barbados, the decline was even more dramatic, moving from about 9,000 in 2013–14 to about 5,700 in 2016–17, according to the latest available UWI Statistical Digest, 2012–13 to 2016–17. The factors contributing to this enrolment decline include government cuts in subsidy for nationals to pursue higher education.

The decline of these two campuses contrasted with the experiences of the Open Campus and the largest campus, Mona (Jamaica). In the case of Open Campus, enrolment in 2013–14 stood at about 6,800, but although 2014–15 saw a sharp decline to approximately 5,600, the campus recovered to within about 100 students of its 2013–14 enrolment, with approximately 6,700 in 2016–17. In the case of Mona, the picture was quite a contrast to the others, with enrolment moving from 16,800 in 2013–14 to just under 18,500 in 2016–17. The factors driving the enrolment numbers at the Open Campus include the convenience of online learning, which is consistent with global trends. There is, however, some irony in the increased enrolment numbers at Mona, as the number of de-registered students had also increased and prompted somewhat of a national and political crisis in May 2017 when the Government of Jamaica announced the intention to pay the outstanding tuition for several final-year students. These students were reportedly facing financial challenges and the risk of not being permitted to sit for final examinations. Disclosures from the university showed that the affected students had been advised of this prospect of being unable to sit for the exams in mid-2016 and had received subsequent reminders.

The declines in enrolment at the UWI are matched by low levels of participation in tertiary education across most countries of the Caribbean. Data from the World Bank (n.d.) show a 27 per cent tertiary participation rate in Jamaica, 25 per cent in Antigua and Barbuda as well as Belize, 19 per cent in Bermuda, 15 per cent in the Bahamas, 14 per cent in St Lucia, 12 per cent for Guyana and 7 per cent in Dominica. These figures are for the years between 2012 and 2017. These levels of participation indicate that there is an urgent need for the UWI as a regional university and Caribbean governments to devise strategies to increase enrolment levels to 60 and 70 per cent, which are typical of developed countries. In this regard Barbados, at 65 per cent, is an outlier in the Caribbean, according to the World Bank. This outlier status would also be applicable to Trinidad and Tobago, according to assertions made by the government in 2014 that as of December 2013, tertiary participation rates were at 65 per cent. The prospects of Caribbean countries, in general, in achieving further increased tertiary enrolment require a reorientation of the mindset of many Caribbean nationals concerning the responsibility of the household for funding tertiary education. Many Caribbean countries cover the cost of their residents accessing tertiary education, and countries have had stops and starts on this issue over the course of the last forty years. In Jamaica, for example, tertiary (and secondary) education was made free in the 1973–74 fiscal year, and this arrangement remained in place until 1986, when a cess was introduced, which effectively ended the practice. Notwithstanding, the government has continued to finance public tertiary education, and thus what students pay represents a fraction of the economic cost of providing the degree based on an 80/20 model. Under this model, the government pays 80 per cent of the economic cost of providing the degree while students pay 20 per cent. But the Government of Jamaica has asserted that even that model is not sustainable and in May 2018 appointed a task force to look at alternative models. The government has also indicated its desire to pursue a policy of treating education loans as mortgages payable over the course of up to thirty years.

Barbados's status as an outlier in terms of the percentage of the population having tertiary education results from the fact that the government covered the full cost of tertiary education for Barbadians. This policy was implemented in 1961 but was suspended in 2013 due to economic austerity. Consequently, enrolment in tertiary institutions fell dramatically; however, the policy was re-instituted in 2017. The realities of financing higher education remain a major challenge for most Caribbean countries, and thus the exploration of approaches to deal with this situation will remain a pressing and urgent necessity for some time to come. One of the challenges which many countries will face, in addition to the challenge of aligning scarce funding to development, is that of cultural expectations of government subsidies and scholarships. These expectations vary in intensity from one country to the next.

Many will ask this lingering question after reflecting on the discussion so far about the funding of tertiary education: "How will governments raise the funding to implement these policy actions?" The answer lies in a very viable but underexplored option: dormant bank accounts. A ready resource from which Caribbean countries can obtain a substantial sum of money which could be used to finance tertiary education, as well as support other efforts at national development, is from the billions of dollars which are sitting in dormant bank accounts.

A 2016 blog entitled "Unclaimed Property in the Caribbean" provides insights on the status of regulations on dormant bank accounts in several jurisdictions and highlights that several Caribbean countries, including Antigua and Barbuda, Bahamas, Barbados, British Virgin Islands, Cayman Islands, Jamaica, St Lucia and Trinidad and Tobago, have substantial deposits of unclaimed assets in commercial banks. These countries also have promulgated regulations governing how these unclaimed assets are to be managed, including how to dispose of said assets. These regulations include provisions for how fees may be levied on such accounts. There is a requirement for commercial banks to notify dormant account holders, provide periodic reports to the Central Bank about the status of these dormant accounts and the period of time that must elapse before those funds may be accessed by the state, which is typically between seven years (as in the case of Cayman) and fifteen years (in the case of Antigua and Jamaica).

Conclusion

The central strategy for the sustainable development of any country must be in its education system. This is a settled question, as the experience of countries across Asia and Europe have shown and as has been discussed in this chapter. The implication therefore is that the sustainable development of the countries of the Caribbean depend on the degree to which they can invest in and leverage the advantages of tertiary-trained graduates. With the low levels of participation in tertiary education, the path to sustainable development for many countries is long and thus urgent steps are needed now to expand enrolment of nationals in tertiary education. One resource for doing so lies in creatively using the billions of dollars these countries have in dormant accounts. While governments seek to take advantage of underused capital, there needs to be more targeted offerings by HEIs, as well as more targeted funding of programmes by government. In addition, there needs to be long-term thinking and planning by both families and the state through the setting aside of small sums of money over time to finance tertiary education later. The model of the Child Trust Fund represents an exciting prospect which would enable governments, with small inputs from parents, to fully fund tertiary education without burdening the budget of the country.

Part 2

Social Activism, Economic
Development, Crime

3.

Social Activism and the Development
of the Caribbean

An examination of the role of academics, or any group in society, raises the fundamental question of ontology. Understood in this manner, such an examination involves an exploration of the role of the academy in the development of any society, and within the context of this book, the role of academics in the development of Caribbean society.

In its ordinary meaning, the notion of activism may be deemed to involve collective efforts to promote a point of view by either advancing a new idea or opposing an existing idea, plan, policy or other movement. Activists are driven by a defined ideology or worldview, and their objective is to seek to ensure that their points of view are considered by decision-makers. The forms in which social activism gets expressed include social media blogs, public gatherings, petitions, street marches, strikes, sit-ins or hunger strikes. Social activism is fuelled by a social movement, and Cammaerts (2015, 2), relying on della Porta and Diani (2006), describes a social movement as a social process through which collective actors articulate their interests, voice grievances and critiques and propose solutions to identified problems by engaging in a variety of collective actions. These movements have three features: (1) they are conflictual and have clearly identified (ideological) opponents; (2) they are structured through dense informal networks; and (3) they are geared towards developing, sustaining and sharing collective identities.

In this chapter, I will seek to examine a bit of the history of social activism in the Caribbean, particularly among academics, and will argue that the level of political consciousness and independence the countries of the Caribbean have experienced in the 1960s and 1970s was due in part to the activism of academics of that generation. I will further argue that in some respects the Caribbean region has experienced a reversal in its political maturity and consciousness and that this is due in large part to the fact that academics and politicians of the current era have lost or lack a sense of political consciousness which informs a Caribbean identity and, in addition, academics are generally no longer involved in social activism.

Historically academics have played a major role in the development of Caribbean institutions, economic structures and processes, sociopolitical and environmental consciousness and the fight for equality and justice. One of the main purposes for which the academy exists, and by extension the university, is the pursuit of justice and the creation of a more nurturing and egalitarian society, which results in improved quality of life and sustainable development. Perspectives on the role and purpose of the university vary, covering the gamut of the utilitarian, the developmental, the philosophical and a mixture of these.

Faust (2010) sees the university as the paramount place for the creation of knowledge and information to advance the development of society, while the popular blog *The Conversation* (Healey 2015) sees the university as preparing students for careers of their choice and enabling them to secure gainful and fulfilling employment. The views of Holten-Andersen (2015) are that while universities have, over the five hundred years since they first came into existence, focused on four main functions – namely being a repository of knowledge, a generator/creator of knowledge, a transferor of knowledge to the next generation and a source of influence in society – they must adopt and vigorously pursue a fifth function. This fifth function is that of being a generator of *economic development* and in this regard play an integral role in furthering economic growth and thereby pursuing socio-economic goals for the whole society. This process inescapably involves contributing to the fight for equality, equity and justice.

The position articulated by Holten-Andersen (2015) is a strong one, and this conclusion is drawn against that background of reflection on the role of academics in the creation of a just and equitable society. In undertaking this reflection, I take account of the findings of Malin and Lubienski (2015), who highlight that a significant amount of the knowledge generated by universities is not accessed as the traditional avenues through which the information is disseminated and is hardly accessed by the people for whom the information is intended. Consideration is also given to Remler (2016), who found that while 88 per cent of research work produced in medicine is cited, only 18 per cent of work produced in the humanities is read. The citation rate for the natural sciences is 73 per cent and the social sciences 68 per cent. The evidence of low levels of utilization or attention paid to the work of academics calls attention to the need to find new ways of bringing knowledge that is generated to the public space and utilizing that knowledge to achieve the ends of a more just and equitable society. One of the questions the current generation of activists should consider today is whether they are doing enough to affect the socio-economic development of their society, and if the answer is "no", which is a reasonable conclusion, then it gives rise to another question: "What more can we do and how should we do it?"

A Synopsis of the Involvement of Caribbean Academics in the Development of the Caribbean

The activism of Caribbean academics peaked in the 1960s and 1970s, with the late Walter Rodney being the premier academic activist, according to Shepherd (2018). Shepherd lists alongside Walter Rodney, Kamau Brathwaite, Lucille Mathurin Mair and Hilary Beckles. According to Shepherd, Rodney shunned the path of the classic intellectual associated traditionally with the ivory tower and snobbishness. According to Shepherd, Rodney saw himself as a shaper of the values and vision of Caribbean society, one grounded in a conviction that it was possible to create a more egalitarian and just society. Alongside the academic activists mentioned by Shepherd, George Beckford, Rex Nettleford and Trevor Munroe of Jamaica; Shridath Ramphal of Guyana; Eugenia Charles of Dominica; Nita Barrows of Barbados; and Arthur Lewis of St Lucia are justifiable additions within the Caribbean region. The following segment presents a summary of the contributions of some of the activists previously named.

George Beckford's seminal contribution, which reflected the thesis of his activism, is contained in his 1972 classic *Persistent Poverty*. This book provided an analysis of the ills of the British plantation system which dominated the Caribbean society and economy and offered a blueprint on how to transform the oppressive planation economies owned by foreigners into world-class economic systems. Entities which are owned by locals and which are involved in the production of finished goods and value-added products, rather than mere exporters of primary products and raw materials, would result in the retention of wealth in Caribbean societies.

Rex Nettleford's (1970) principal work *Mirror Mirror* provides a deep analysis of social and racial tensions in Jamaican society, though relevant to other Caribbean societies, and makes the case that cohesion is an absolute imperative for national survival and development. Nettleford sought to give verve and vitality to his vision of a more cohesive society by engaging the arts, and pursuant to this founded, directed and served as the principal choreographer of the renowned National Dance Theatre Company of Jamaica.

Shridath Ramphal, who served as the second secretary-general of the British Commonwealth (1975–90), is a legal luminary and intellectual who sought to fulfil the mandate of creating a West Indian (Caribbean) integration movement which could be used to foster the development of the Caribbean. He also served as the assistant attorney general of the West Indian Federation (1958–62). His passion for West Indian integration was deep, and with the political dismantling of the federation resulting from the withdrawal of one of the ten countries, Ramphal sought to build an organic integration movement based on the shared values of human progress and the need to restore the Caribbean economy and build a Caribbean identity. His philosophy was that the West Indies (which he called "we") was both a geographical and a philosophical identity construct and that it was only as the Caribbean nations acted in concert with each other to pursue their collective destiny that each would experience real progress. Ramphal's vision of an integrated Caribbean and the work he has done to achieve this remain his most compelling contribution as an academic activist.

Trevor Munroe is a Jamaican political scientist and labour activist. His early foray into activism inspired him to lead the founding of the University and Allied Workers Union, an entity which remains an active voice in Jamaica's labour movement. Munroe led the University and Allied Workers Union for several years, and having built a sustainable structure, handed over leadership to the second tier of leaders. Munroe also co-founded and led for several years the Workers' Party of Jamaica, a left-leaning political party which adopted an aggressive advocacy and activist posture in seeking to promote socio-economic equality in Jamaica.

Both the University and Allied Workers Union and the Workers' Party of Jamaica provided technical and logical support to other workers' movements in the Caribbean. Munroe's (1972) activist agenda, which sought to give the worker a greater voice, was founded in large measure on the thesis of his doctoral dissertation, *The Politics of Constitutional Decolonization,* which he completed at the young age of twenty-eight. In the years prior to his retirement from the university, Munroe founded yet another movement, National Integrity Action, which is an advocacy organization that is committed to promoting good governance and ending corruption.

In sum, these Caribbean activist stalwarts made significant contributions to their respected countries, with some even extending influence to the wider Caribbean. Beckford's approach to activism may be described as strategic, structural and rooted in economic advocacy. On the other hand, Nettleford's enactment of activism may be described as mild and congenial and rooted in cultural advocacy; in stark contrast to Nettleford, Rodney's activism may be described as communal, organizational, oppositional and even aggressive. Ramphal's integrationist pursuits may be characterized as diplomatic activism, while Munroe's could be marked as political, labour and good governance activism. Despite their varied approaches, the compelling lesson readers should not miss is that each of these scholars brought their tremendous intellectual weight to bear on engagement on the ground in pursuit of a better society – a task not external to the reach of current academics.

The demonstration of their firm commitment to activism resonates with the reflections of Adam Kuper (1976), who in the book *Changing Jamaica,* explains that his aim is to sketch a total analysis of contemporary Jamaican society and in the process suggest ways in which the various facets of society – the political, economic and social – are articulated with each other. He concludes, however, that while success in such an endeavour is a hopeless task and one for which he is ill equipped, it is a task that nonetheless must be undertaken if the academy is to move from being merely academic and distanced from the harsh and complex issues which bedevil society. Kuper seems to hold the view that academics need not have all "the how-to" answers to act; they should be undaunted by what seems impossible to achieve and they should resist the urge to remain complacent and satisfied by being a mere academic. Instead, they should commit their lives to representing those issues that have the potential to change undesirable human conditions. The example offered through the advocacy agenda of the foregoing scholars, in my view, demonstrates the beauty and power of transforming intellectual ferment into social change.

Social Activism in the Twenty-First Century

The level of activism which characterized the 1960s and 1970s has waned and the creation of a deeper level of social consciousness which it sought to create has not been realized. But the involvement of Caribbean academics in social activism in the 1960s was not unique to the Caribbean. There was the famous student movement of the 1960s in America which sought to address issues such as civil rights, poverty and liberating college students. That movement turned its attention to protesting the Vietnam War in the second half of that decade. In Latin America there was the movement to overthrow oppression and American hegemony, which gave birth to liberation theology. A similar movement in North America gave birth to black theology, which sought to end white domination of the Christian church. A parallel and independent development was the feminist movement, which, among other things, gave birth to feminist theology. The feminist movement also played a key role in the legislation on abortion in America, which is encapsulated in the now-threatened law *Roe v. Wade*.

Since the late 1980s there has been a decline in social activism among academics, and it was not until the 2000s that the protest movement regained urgency with undertakings such as the 2010 protests in the United Kingdom, mass protests against the Trump administration (starting the day of his inauguration in 2017) and student protests in France in April 2018 and the gas riots in that country in November 2018. The most successful mobilization involving academics was the student protest "March for Our Lives" in March 2018 in which almost three-quarters of the participants (72 per cent) were persons with bachelor's degrees. There was also a protest led by teachers in Kentucky who were protesting cuts to the education budget of that state, given its implications for students. Both "March for Our Lives" and the teachers' protests in Kentucky were examples of expressions of social consciousness demanding change.

While other countries and regions have seen high levels of social activism recently, countries of the Caribbean and the Caribbean as a whole have not witnessed any major, large-scale activism by academics since the 1980s. Some segments of Caribbean societies have shown interest in public issues, and there have been debates on social media, as well as a growing trend of feminist advocacy, for example, using social media to advance various women's causes. However, there has not been the kind of organized activism of the likes of the 1960s and 1970s or of the kind seen in 2017 and 2018 in the United Kingdom, France and the United States.

The absence of strong intellectual ferment translating to social action is an issue which warrants further study. Reitz (2016) in his book *Philosophy and Critical Pedagogy: Insurrection and Commonwealth,* provides a simple exposition that could help to elucidate why there have not been strong activist movements among intellectuals. Locating his analysis within the context of the education sector, Reitz (2016) highlights the propensity of governments to exploit the vulnerabilities of workers and to engage in divide-and-rule tactics. He suggests that the economic wants of workers make them vulnerable to exploitation. Academics such as teachers, who are placed in financially impecunious positions, have difficulty (the rare Kentucky example aside) focusing on any other issue but survival. This exploitation of workers, Reitz opines, is part of a larger project of political subjugation which is practised on the unschooled. The need for social consciousness, which acts as a barrier to exploitation, has been articulated by Karl Marx, who reasoned that the end of the system of exploitation which characterized nineteenth-century societies would only be realized when the working class acquired the consciousness to move from being merely a class in itself to becoming a class for itself.

An Example of Government Exploitation of Vulnerabilities

The analysis offered by Reitz (2016) and the need for the antidote described by Marx provide an excellent backdrop for understanding an example of government exploitation of workers' vulnerability and how such exploitation contributes to the dampening of the activist spirit. The following example which is used to illustrate how government exploits the vulnerable is drawn from the Jamaican context.

Between 2016 and 2018, Jamaican teachers were engaged in negotiations with the government for a new contract period. For the better part of two years not much happened, despite efforts by the teachers' union to get the government to start negotiations. Towards the end of the second year, with not much time left before the financial year 2017–18 expired, the government began to show seeming urgency to negotiate. But in reality, what was happening was that the government was seeking to use the excuse of "time is running out" to back the teachers into a corner. The teachers would be eager to settle and get an increase in the paltry salary many of them receive. This was a classic example of the exploitation of vulnerabilities of workers of which Reitz speaks.

Bought for the Price of a Patty

To expand this idea, the cheapest patty in Jamaica is about J$150. A patty is a small meat (or vegetable) filled crust usually three inches wide and five inches long. It is not a full meal; its cost is equivalent to the value of what teachers of Jamaica have received in their capitulation to the government in their 2017–21 wage negotiations. Examination of the heads of agreement between the Jamaica Teachers' Association (JTA) and the Jamaican government was quite illuminating. It revealed that the retroactive payments that the JTA agreed to accept translates to J$55,549 before tax at the first point on an eleven-point scale for the trained graduate. At the second point on the scale it is J$56,771; it is J$61,935 at the sixth point and J$69,054.00 at the highest (eleventh) point. Thus, the teacher at the eleventh and highest point received J$69,054 before taxes for the period April 2017 to March 2018. This translates to J$5,754.50 per month, or J$191.81 per day, and settles at J$134.27 after taxes, which is less than the price of the cheapest patty – for the highest-paid teacher.

The negotiations did not fare any better for school principals, either. There are four categories of secondary schools in Jamaica, which are classified as grades I to IV, with IV being the highest category. A grade IV secondary school typically has a teaching staff of eighty to one hundred, support staff (ancillary, academic, administrative) of up to fifty and a student population of up to two thousand. The principal of such a school, who is at the top of the scale, earns about J$2.8 million. The 5 per cent amounts to J$140,000 more per annum, or J$11,666 per month, before taxes, and thus J$388 per day. After taxes, the net increase is J$273, which is about the price of the most expensive patty. That is what the highest-paid principal of a secondary school received at the end of the cunningly managed salary negotiations.

Although the teachers had initially voted on three occasions to reject the offer, the government decided to go ahead and pay the retroactive portion based on the percentage offer it had made. The decision of the government to proceed to implement the wage increase, which the teachers voted by a large majority to reject, is a classic example of divide and rule. The method is that those who comply are pulled into a relationship of patronage but are constantly reminded, even subtly, that if they secede from the relationship, there could be grave consequences, and therein is one element of instilling fear. In this regard the government has played on the vulnerabilities of some teachers.

Given the minuscule offer that was on the table, the JTA could have used its negotiations to demonstrate their self-understanding as a group of philosophers of education and educational policy implementers. They could have shown how they position themselves in a conversation with the government about the place of its members in advancing the interests of society. However, it is clear that the JTA, in accepting that low salary increase, missed an opportunity to contribute to the betterment of their members. But are they aware of how they could have achieved this end?

JTA and Their Advocacy Role

There is anecdotal evidence suggesting that the JTA is perceived as having salary negotiations as its primary role. It appears that many members of the JTA do not see that there is a bigger issue at stake – namely its role as an advocacy group to advance the quality of education in the country. The execution of this role of pursuing the betterment of education in the country is complementary to, not in competition with, its role of seeking to advance the interests of its members. The JTA, as the single largest group of educators, has a duty to be a force for the transformation of education in Jamaica; but it has not been as vocal as it ought to be on issues affecting the education sector. The apparent surrender of the JTA and its failure to engage in a real fight over ideas, principles and processes runs counter to the spirit for which the union is known. Hewitt (2012) reflects on this spirit, describing it as a spirit of struggle. Hewitt argues that the JTA, from its inception, had to fight against the attempt to make teachers civil servants, as well as attempts to divide teachers. He contends that the strength of the union lay in cooperative efforts and that it faced awesome vulnerability once divided. However, they are not alone in this regard.

The shortcomings of the JTA are not unique; they are typical of the shortcomings of the academic community generally, which has failed to be a vocal force that challenges issues of deficits in the education system but also confronts issues of leadership, corruption, public waste, poor governance and lack of accountability in the wider national sphere. These vulnerabilities are not factors over which the JTA's members have control, but these exist in part because of the lack of the class consciousness of which Karl Marx was concerned when he analysed the issues facing workers.

4.

Sustainable Economic Development
The Centrality of Education

The Jamaican economy has experienced unprecedented stability over the last five years, 2013–18, with the economy recording growth in every fiscal quarter, as reported by the Planning Institute of Jamaica. Despite the level of stability experienced, real GDP growth has averaged less than 1 per cent. The stability in the economy, which began in 2013, has resulted in part from support by the World Bank, the International Monetary Fund and the Inter-American Development Bank, which have provided policy development and investment financing to support private-sector-led growth, public-sector transformation and building social and climate resilience, according the 2018 World Bank (2019) report on Jamaica.

The Goal of Economic Development

In this chapter I examine the issue of economic growth in Jamaica and argue the case that although the country has been experiencing a sustained period of growth, albeit meagre (at an average of 1 per cent per annum) the fact of GDP growth alone, and the relative stability it signifies, are not enough to transform the country to developed country status or even to guarantee improved living conditions for the majority. The chapter closes with a return to the theme of education and its role in contributing to sustained economic growth.

The discussion on education in this chapter, within the context of the broader discussion on sustainable economic development, constitutes the centrepiece of this book. The issues examined are related to the opening discussion in chapter 1, which examines the threat to the viability and survival of HEIs in the Caribbean as a result of the creation of a borderless world which is sanctioned by the GATS. The issues in this chapter also connect to the discussion in chapter 2, which explores various approaches to financing higher education. The argument that is being made here, which is premised on chapters 1 and 2, is that the goal of sustainable economic development for the Caribbean can only be realized through education. The realization of this goal requires a thriving, relevant and responsive higher education system and governments that are committed to finding ways to fund higher education. While the discussion in this chapter is largely focused on Jamaica, the issues are also relevant to the Caribbean as a whole.

This chapter is also connected to the issue of activism, which is discussed in chapter 3. The argument I make in the alignment of chapters 3 and 4 is that the responsiveness of Caribbean leaders to the call to position education as the path to sustainable economic development will depend, in part, on the vigour of the advocacy of academics. In the chapters which follow in this second part of the book, starting with chapter 5, and all four chapters of part 3, I highlight certain dangers to the project of attaining economic sustainable development. In chapter 5 I examine a common enemy to the Caribbean – crime – using Jamaica as a case study, and in chapters 6 to 9 I explore issues related to leadership and institutional development. The basic argument is that if countries of the Caribbean are to experience sustainable economic development, leadership will have to be courageous and corruption free and our public institutions will have to be transformed.

Economic Growth in Jamaica

The World Bank's (2019) report of 2018 notes that Jamaica's GDP grew by about 0.5 per cent in 2017, which represented a significant decline when compared to the 1.4 per cent in 2016. This decline was due largely to severe floods and other adverse weather conditions during the first half of 2017. Despite this, the country's macroeconomic indicators are all heading in the right direction – low inflation, large net international reserves, low interest rates, reduction in the public debt and political stability. There are other fruits being reaped from the economic reforms, which began in 2013 with the highest levels of employment in fifty years, but at the same time more people falling below the poverty line in 2017, compared to 2015, according to figures put out by the Statistical Institute of Jamaica.

Despite the praiseworthy macroeconomic stability and having attained GDP growth of 1.4 per cent in 2016, 2017 was 0.5 per cent, 2018 at 1.7 per cent and 2019 projected to be 0.7 per cent, the overall picture of Jamaica's economic position is one of low growth. An examination of the history of economic growth in Jamaica since 1980 is presented in table 4.1.

One way of reading the data in table 4.1 is to conclude that over the twenty years, 1980–99, growth was an average of 1.35 per cent and 2.32 per cent in each ten-year period, with fifteen of those years recording growth. By comparison, growth averaged 0.53 per cent and 0.88 per cent in the subsequent twenty years with also fifteen of those years recording growth. The

Table 4.1. Jamaica's GDP Growth Performance 1980–2018

Period	Mean GDP Growth	Year(s)/Highest Growth	Year(s)/Lowest Growth	Number of Years of Positive Growth
1980–89	2.32%	1987 7.7%	1980 and 1988 –4%	7
1990–99	1.35%	1990 4.9%	1997 –1.6%	8
2000–9	0.88%	2003 3.7%	2009 –3.4%	8 (both years of negative growth were the recession years of 2008 and 2009)
2010–18	0.53%	2016 1.5%	2010 –1.4%	7

inescapable conclusion is that while there have been some spectacular growth years, such as 1987, and taking account of the subsequent trends, 2003, our growth performance has been generally weak. Another way of reading the data is to observe that the average rate of growth in each period is remarkably lower than in the previous period. The big question we must therefore ask is: What is the explanation for the anaemic economic growth being experienced (external shocks such as flooding aside), despite the stable macroeconomic environment in which we operate? I submit that the answer to this question lies in our culture of lack of productivity, which in part has its roots in our education system.

Refocusing Measurements of Economic Growth

Whenever the Planning Institute of Jamaica gives its quarterly reports on the economy, it typically reports on performance in the areas of

- agriculture
- mining and quarrying
- manufacturing
- construction
- electricity and water supply
- transport, storage and communication
- wholesale and retail and the installation and repair of machinery
- finance and insurance services
- hotels and restaurants

What is glaringly missing from this list, because they are not measured, are education and training, the creative industries, youth entrepreneurship, health and wellness and technology innovation. While there is potential for sustainable growth in the traditional areas, particularly agriculture, manufacturing and finance and insurance services, growth in the other sectors is not likely to be significant.

John Csiszar, in a 30 July 2019 article entitled "Ten Fastest-Growing Industries to Invest in This Year", cited global research firm IBIS World which lists among the fastest-growing industries in 2019 sectors such as finance (savings and thrift), the environment and technology applications, specifically e-commerce and online transactions, in tenth, ninth and eighth positions, respectively. Internet publishing and broadcasting was placed in the third position and solar power in second. Warfare equipment, which may be hardly relevant to Jamaica, is in third position, but while not relevant to Jamaica is a story on its own.

The findings of Csiszar's 2019 piece are somewhat corroborated by a 9 July 2018 report in *World Finance Magazine* which lists the five fastest-growing world industries as renewable energy, cybersecurity, biotechnology, virtual reality and artificial intelligence. While the specifics of both lists may differ somewhat, the common themes knitting them together are technology and the environment. It is striking that in both lists, and in both themes, we can locate the three areas which arguably represent potential sustainable growth areas for Jamaica, namely agriculture (environment), manufacturing (biotechnology and artificial intelligence) and finance and insurance services (finance, cybersecurity, e-commerce and online transactions). Refocusing on growth will require investment by the government in areas of study which are aligned to these growth areas. It will also require that HEIs develop short- (a few weeks) and medium- (a few months) length programmes to complement their regular two- and three-year degree programmes to provide citizens with the skills and competencies to take advantage of the economic opportunities which are available in the areas listed.

Macroeconomic Stability Is Not an End in Itself

One of the mistakes successive political administrations in Jamaica have made is that of seemingly conceiving of macroeconomic stability as an end in itself rather than a means to an end (or various ends). It is almost trite logic, but an overlooked fact, that macroeconomic stability is not intended to protect the private sector or insulate the poor against hardships or enable the state to fund social protection programmes when hardships occur. Macroeconomic stability is to be pursued as a means of stimulating increased production and higher levels of productivity across all areas of the economy.

Jamaica can learn quite a bit from other countries which have successfully pursued macroeconomic stability but have not attained significant economic growth. Mexico is a good example of this. Employees of the Ministry of Finance in Mexico, José Córdova and Juan Padilla, in a 2016 article entitled *Productivity in Mexico: Trends, Drivers and Institutional Framework*, argue that while Mexico is the poster child for the implementation of economic policies that should foster strong, economic and stable growth, economic growth in that country has been lacklustre. The country's real GDP growth has averaged 2.4 per cent between 1980 and 2014, according to Córdova and Padilla.

They suggest that among the strategies undertaken in the Government of Mexico by successive political administrations to achieve macroeconomic stability are making the Central Bank autonomous, reducing the public deficit and establishing new rules which guarantee responsible management of public finances. It also took steps which saw the Mexican government transitioning to a flexible exchange rate and pursuing a policy of low inflation. The resulting macroeconomic stability stimulated reductions in the cost of credit (interest rates on loans) and increased foreign investment, especially after Mexico's entry into the North American Free Trade Agreement in 1994, Córdova and Padilla indicate.

All of the measures taken by Mexico have been adopted by Jamaica, and the signs are there to show that Jamaica is experiencing macroeconomic stability. Additionally, Jamaica and Mexico both share the experience of low economic growth despite macroeconomic stability. Mexico's average GDP growth of 2.4 per cent between 1980 and 2014 (which is much greater than Jamaica's) is about half the average of 4.6 per cent experienced by emerging and developing economies, according to the Asian Productivity Report. The reason advanced by Córdova and Padilla for Mexico's low GDP growth, despite unprecedented macroeconomic stability, is weak multifactor productivity growth. The most recent figures on GDP growth in Mexico show 2 per cent in 2017, which is lower than the average of the previous thirty-four years. The April–June quarter of 2018 has shown shrinkage of 0.1 per cent. The chief factor responsible for this latest performance, the first since 2015, was a decline in productivity levels, particularly agriculture.

So ultimately, while macroeconomic stability is good, right and necessary, in and of itself and by itself, it does not make for an improved quality of life for the majority, nor does it by itself improve productivity. The experience of our not-too-distant geographical neighbour, Mexico, has proven this. Thus, our success at creating and maintaining macroeconomic stability does not address many of the difficult economic challenges faced by low-wage and middle-income workers and the implications of these challenges to meet healthcare costs and tuition fees. There is need, therefore, for a more robust relationship between the pursuit and preservation of macroeconomic stability and the positioning, partitioning and planning of our education system for macroeconomic stability and productivity (both multifactor and labour) to go hand in hand.

Jamaica's Productivity Profile Compared

Brian Wynter, then governor of the Bank of Jamaica, in a September 2011 speech entitled "Productivity in Jamaica" noted that total factor productivity (also known as multifactor productivity) had declined at a rate of 2.1 per cent over the twenty-year period from 1990 to 2010. Labour productivity (output per worker) had also declined by 0.5 per cent over the same period, resulting in economic growth between 2000 and 2010 averaging 0.8 per cent compared to a rate of 2.6 per cent per year of our Caribbean neighbours. As shown earlier, our economic growth continues to be in the region of 1 per cent per year or less.

By contrast, the productivity and economic growth of countries in Asia and Europe have seen increases. The Asian Productivity Organization, in its 2016 Productivity Databook, asserts that countries in that region experienced economic growth of between 5.4 per cent and 5.7 per cent over the period 2010–14, while China's growth slowed to 7.8 per cent during the same period.

In relation to labour productivity, the Asian Productivity Organization found that between 2005 and 2014 China's labour productivity grew by 9 per cent, while Myanmar's and Mongolia's grew by 7.8 per cent and 7.2 per cent, respectively. These rates of growth in productivity per worker compare with declines in Jamaica. Among the factors to which economic growth and productivity in Asia have been attributed are the availability of capital, the structure of industries, industry diversification, forecasting of and focusing on key areas for growth and the base structure of a skills-leaning education system. If Jamaica is therefore to experience sustainable economic growth and development, it must attend to the issues of the availability of capital to small and micro industries; it must pursue a wider range of industry opportunities, consistent with the direction of global growth; and it must invest heavily in education, both in strengthening the base (the early childhood and primary levels) and in higher education.

In relation to the last two factors, one country that has shown tremendous creativity and reaped great success is India. India has shifted its economy and education system to one which focuses on services and skill development. This in part explains its membership in the emerging economic and financial power known as the BRICS (Brazil, Russia, India, China and South Africa). India's annual GDP growth was 7.71 per cent in 2016, with a labour productivity rate averaging 4.95 per cent between December 1992 and December 2017, according to the Asian Productivity Report. One obvious lesson from this is the need to increase the number of participants in higher education, who by virtue of their higher skills are able to engage in value-added provision of services. This means that HEIs need to review their programme offerings so as to ensure that they are equipping graduates with competencies which enable them to up the value chain.

Services: The Expanding Frontier in Economic Growth

The growth in GDP and labour productivity being experienced by countries in Asia, as well as India, as discussed earlier, is not only attributable to the design of their education systems but to their focus on transforming primary products into value-added consumer products, as well as on services. Forty-five years ago, the late George Beckford, the activist who was discussed in chapter 3 and author of the book *Persistent Poverty*, recommended that if the former planation economies of the Caribbean were to overcome persistent poverty, their economic model had to be changed from being merely exporters of raw materials and primary products to exporters of value-added, high-end goods and the provider of services. If Jamaica is to experience meaningful GDP growth, its government and other economic policymakers must heed the timeless advice of Beckford.

Jamaica's trade deficit in 2017 was US$4.38 billion. A country's trade deficit is the difference between the total value of its imports and its exports. This statistic means that Jamaica imported US$4.38 billion worth of goods and services more than that it exported. This figure of $4.38 billion also represents the average (mean) of the ten-year period 2008–17. During the period there were four years during which the deficit fell below the US$4 billion mark and five in which it was in the US$4 billion range (US$4.4 to US$4.82). As long as Jamaica continues to produce low levels of GDP growth (which has averaged about 1 per cent for the last forty years) while at the same time importing so much more than we export, most of our people will experience diminished quality of life. The solution to this back-straining trade deficit is the expansion of the service sector.

The term "service sector" is sometimes used in reference to services such as barbers, waiters, drivers, cooks and technicians. While the services offered by these providers have the potential to improve personal income and increase economic activity at some levels of society, their capacity to contribute to long-term sustainable development is limited. The *Groningen Growth and Development Centre* in the Netherlands has found that the top five intermediate global services in highest demand are transport, storage and communication, financial, real estate and business services. Adilson Giovanini and Marcelo Arend (2017) of the University of Brazil articulate the depth and complexity of a value-added service sector in developed economies and its relationship to higher education. They note that developed economies manufacture increasingly more sophisticated products that require an increased amount of knowledge. In this context, industrial-sector productivity growth is characterized by its diversification, which includes low technological intensity products to higher-level, more complex products, and at each stage, increasing volumes of knowledge are required.

Craft vending is a popular trade in Jamaica. When a craft vendor shapes a piece of wood into a doll using a carving knife, he or she is applying a certain level of knowledge to add value to a primary product. The same tree that is used to make a wooden doll can be used to make various forms of writing paper, but the process of transformation requires a more advanced level of knowledge from the farming process of tree planting, to cutting, transportation to the factory and the chemical engineering process of turning the wood into pulp and the pulp into paper. It is in these respects that service becomes the frontier of economic development. Interestingly, the said craft vendor could become a more astute, efficient and economically prosperous craft entrepreneur by drawing on a higher level of knowledge and manufacturing dozens or hundreds of wooden dolls per day and selling not only in Fern Gully but some sort of Silicon Valley where exotic dolls which look a certain way are in demand.

It is not without profound significance that among the top five most productive countries (Luxembourg, Norway, Switzerland, Denmark and Iceland) are two countries which are most effective in leveraging human capital, namely, Norway and Switzerland, which rank at number two and three, respectively, on the Human Capital Leveraging Index (World Economic Forum 2015b). The other three countries in the top five of the index are Finland at number one and Canada and Japan at positions four and five, respectively, according to the 2018 *Gazette Review* (Jones 2018). It is equally instructive that the length of the work week in the top four most productive countries is 29.75 hours, with Norway having a 27-hour work week. Norway is an outlier at 48 hours, including maximum allowed overtime. This fact confirms a basic concept of productivity: that it is output per hour which counts, not the number of hours one spends at work. These findings again confirm the critical role that value-added services will play in the attainment of economic development, and this will only be realized if there is an education system which is producing graduates who are highly productive.

The Devaluation of the Jamaican Dollar

Successive governments have used various methods to combat the devaluation and its consequences. For example, it has been touted that the former prime minister of Jamaica, Edward Seaga, is said to have zealously guarded the dollar and, according to some analysts, he kept it artificially low during his reign from October 1980 to February 1989. The Bank of Jamaica's "Historic Rates of the Jamaican Dollar to the US Dollar" report shows that the Jamaican dollar, having remained in the region of J$5.50 to US$1 from late 1985 to mid-1989, entered the J$5.60 range later that year, and in October 1989 reached the J$6:US$1 mark. In early 1990, it reached J$7:US$1 and by the middle of March 1991 was trading at over J$9:US$1. With the frightening J$10:US$1 mark approaching, the society was in a panic. After a few weeks of respite via revaluation, the official J$10:US$1 mark was reached 24 May 1991, when the dollar traded at J$10.31 to US$1. Thus, having remained in the J$5.50:US$1 region for over four years to late 1989, the rate of exchange doubled in two years. In another six months, by the end of November 1991, the J$20:US$1 mark was reached and the society was in full crisis mode.

Businesses which did not earn US dollars but had to purchase goods using US dollars were at a distinct disadvantage, as they needed an increasing number of Jamaican dollars to buy the US dollars. In a similar vein, the country's US dollar debt became more and more expensive to service with every upward movement in the dollar, as more Jamaican dollars were required to purchase US dollars to service the debt. The outcome for the consumer, with merchants having to spend more dollars on goods, was obvious price increases. These consequences spread across all areas of the economy when fuel prices rise and the dollar devalues. By the time the dollar broke the dreaded J$100:US$1 mark in June 2013, society was numb. A year later, when the dollar was trading at J$111:US$1, the then leader of the opposition, Andrew Holness, saw the situation as a major crisis. So strong was his concern that he wrote to the head of the International Monetary Fund, who was on a visit to Jamaica, to convey his concerns. A news report carried in the *Jamaica Observer* dated 27 June 2014 quotes a Jamaica Labour Party press release as expressing the opposition's concerns on the devaluation of the dollar, citing the need to build stability in the Jamaican economy and the challenges which ordinary Jamaicans are experiencing as a result of the movement of the Jamaican dollar.

With that background, should the movement of the dollar from J$122.45:US$1 in April 2016 to J$135.59 in August 2018 and J$142:US$1 in November 2019 be a cause for concern? Former minister of finance Peter Phillips had argued for a market-determined rate of the dollar in response to the (then) opposition's demand for action to keep the dollar from reaching J$120:US$1, and minister of finance Nigel Clarke called for an end to the practice of playing politics with the devaluation of the dollar. In response to the devaluations in 2019, the party in opposition has called for action to protect the dollar.

Two classic reasons are given by governments who favour currency devaluation: (1) it boosts exports because the cost of the country's goods falls and (2) it shrinks the deficit, as imports become more expensive and so people consume fewer foreign goods. There is no evidence that either of these strategies has worked in Jamaica. The position of the opposition spokesman on finance, Mark Golding, as reported in the *Jamaica Observer Newspaper* of 28 October 2019, is that the fluctuations in the price of the dollar were having an adverse impact on households and businesses.

It is clear from the contrasting and seemingly evolving or revised positions of the political parties while in government versus while in opposition that the political versus social and economic issues of devaluation need to be disentangled. It is inescapable that devaluation has adverse impacts on purchasing power, and those who earn a fixed or low income will be adversely affected. There is consensus that the solution lies in greater productivity, but that increased productivity cannot be realized when 70 per cent of workers do not have the kind of training to undertake service activities and where most jobs being created are low-end jobs. This reality highlights the urgent need for radical reforms to the education system.

Corruption and the Impact on the Economy

Transparency International defines corruption as the abuse of entrusted power for private gain. This gain can be financial and non-financial. The World Economic Forum (2015a), in a report entitled "How Does Corruption Affect Economic Growth?", asserts that corruption is a major hindrance to economic growth and has a corrosive impact on the fabric of society. The World Bank has made similar assertions, noting that the impact on the private sector is also considerable, as it distorts competition and is estimated to add 10 per cent or more to the costs of doing business in many parts of the world. Therefore, corruption can be assumed to have a significant deleterious impact on any economy. Following is an assessment of Jamaica's experiences with corruption and its impact on the economy. Hector Boham and Sam Rockson Asamoah, in a 2011 article, discuss ten ways in which corruption hampers economic development. Heading the list are higher consumer prices, reduced investments and the consequential reduction in available goods and services. This results in inflation, reduced foreign direct investment and a reduced ability of the government to provide vital services as budgets are underfunded. The International Monetary Fund estimates that corruption deprives the Jamaican economy of 5 per cent of GDP. If governance in Jamaica were to reach a point of probity, transparency and fairness and was able to reduce corruption to 1 per cent of GDP, it would be a great legacy. That would add about 4 per cent GDP growth. Additionally, if corruption were significantly reduced, it could spur a level of economic activity that would be unprecedented. Countries such as New Zealand, Singapore and Finland, which have low levels of corruption, experience high levels of economic growth, and the correlation between both has been affirmed by the International Monetary Fund, the World Bank and Transparency International.

Any government should treat addressing the malady of corruption as urgent because of the social and economic implications for its citizenry. Corruption is the main reason for public apathy and mistrust of politicians and political parties. Election campaign spending is a major avenue for corrupt activity, and political parties have often sought to sanitize election spending by focusing on infrastructure. The experience of Jamaica has been that many of the assets produced by those projects do not last long. But given the undeniable stranglehold that corruption has on society and the economy, I submit that a major focus of political leadership should be ending corruption. The following recommendations are advanced for policy considerations:

1. Require parliamentarians to publicly disclose their assets and earnings and that of members of their families (rather than merely filing a report on those assets with the Integrity Commission) upon entering public office and for each year while in office.
2. Enforce legislation which prevents public officials from securing personal favours through their public office (kickbacks and other forms of illicit enrichment).
3. Empower Tax Administration Jamaica to shine the spotlight on, and send the Revenue Protection Division after, public officials who evade or avoid paying taxes, in the same way ordinary citizens and entrepreneurs are pressured by the Tax Administration Jamaica.
4. Pass legislation prohibiting politicians from dodging tax obligations by taking money earned in Jamaica and investing it overseas.

The net effect of these measures will be increased transparency of the financial affairs of public officials and thus the potential for reduced likelihood of their being involved in corrupt financial activities.

Placing Jamaica's Economic Growth in Context

The Elixir: Higher Education

The strategy which holds the key to sustainable economic growth is education, and specifically higher education. For any country to leverage the advantages for growth in the present and likely future areas of growth, such a country must have a first-rate education system with 80 per cent of the graduates from high school going into tertiary education. In simple terms, it requires highly trained university graduates (who possess degrees in the sciences, mathematics, economics, finance, the environment, and so on, backed by adequate exposure to ethics, law and leadership) to sustainably grow an economy. Wan-hua Ma (2003) points to the correlation between education and economic development, noting that the essence of the relationship between the Chinese economy and its education system is that the latter prepares research personnel, business leaders and entrepreneurs; provides small business support; invents cutting-edge technologies and business development innovations; develops new products and services; and provides investment assistance.

The lack of growth in the Jamaican economy in the more than forty years since secondary and tertiary education was opened up to the masses, thanks to the educational policies of the 1970s, is largely attributable to fundamental weaknesses in our education system. Ours is not an education system which promotes creativity, self-reliance, collaboration and the value of owning one's business. On the contrary, the system stifles creativity, supports dependence (rather than interdependence), glorifies self-defeating competition rather than collaboration and praises getting a job rather than creating one.

Wan-hua Ma, in a 2003 article entitled "Economic Reform and Higher Education in China", traces the parallel developments of the Chinese economy and tertiary education system. Ma notes that 1976 marked a turning point in China's political, economic and higher education philosophies. With respect to its political and economic philosophies, China shifted focus from privatization of enterprises to the creation of new enterprises and from promoting property rights to promoting market competition. In relation to its higher education philosophy, the developments were phenomenal, as discussed earlier, wherein the number of HEIs in China has increased by 6.6 times in the forty-year period between 1976 and 2016, from 392 in 1976 to a whopping 2,596 as of 2016.

With that phenomenal level of expansion in China's education system, Ma cites many examples of the impact on Chinese society and economy. Their success in solving local food shortage and feeding 22 per cent of the world's population with less than 7 per cent of the world's farmlands reflects creativity and ingenuity in planning and effective execution. Ma notes further that some ten years after the reform of its higher education system in 1976, annual GDP growth in China was 11.8 per cent in 1988; in 1993, the annual growth rate peaked at 13.4 per cent but fell sharply to 9.0 per cent in 1997 and fell further to 7.8 per cent in 2002. In the quarter of a century between 1977 and 2002, China has experienced annual average GDP growth of 9.4 per cent. Though its growth has slowed considerably since, falling by about 50 per cent, China continues to be the fastest-growing economy, with its 2017 rate of growth being 6.8 per cent, slowing to 6.4 per cent in 2018, and 6.1 per cent in 2019, and projected to be even slower to 5.9 per cent in 2020, before the onslaught of the deadly COVID-19 pandemic.

Mi Zhou and Louis Vaccaro, in a 2007 paper entitled "Strengthening the Relationship between Higher Education and Regional Economic Development", point to the correlation between education and economic development, noting that the essence of the relationship between the Chinese economy and its education system is that the latter prepares research personnel, business leaders and entrepreneurs and provides small business support.

Therefore, the vitality and value of higher education to economic growth is so self-evident that it is almost mind-boggling that successive political administrations in Jamaica have done so little to radically address the deficits in the pre-tertiary sector. Densil Williams (2019), professor of international business, who is responsible for strategic planning at the UWI, in a newspaper article entitled "More Prosperity, More Poverty", cites this problem, highlighting the fact that of the 1.3 million people in the Jamaican workforce, more than 900,000, or about 70 per cent, do not have certification beyond the primary and secondary level. This means, as Williams explains, that not only will 70 per cent of the workforce be forced to subsist off low-paying wages but their ability to contribute to economic growth is minimal. Thus, when, for example, the Planning Institute of Jamaica reports that substantial numbers of persons have found employment in the wholesale and retail section and in the installation and repair of machinery sector, it only confirms Williams's findings. It confirms the dire reality of Jamaicans in terms of how a lack of education affects the poor and marginalized; it also indicates that Jamaican politicians and educational stakeholders are ignorant of the role that education plays in achieving economic goals and that urgent thought must be given to the education system, with the aim of redesigning it to catalyse and maximize economic growth. I contend that in a knowledge era, a country should not be celebrating the fact that qualified high school graduates have landed minimum-wage jobs.

Brent Radcliffe, in a 28 July 2019 article entitled "How Education and Training Affect the Economy", reminds readers of some basic facts, such as the relationship between an excess supply of workers working in industries with low entry requirements. The result will be low wages. This is the reality being lived by high school graduates who serve as pump attendants, cashiers, chamber maids and porters, with the minimum entry requirement being between three and five Caribbean Examinations Council subjects. Persons holding these jobs are not producing or selling a product or providing a service of high value. According to Radcliffe, it is beyond dispute that the education and training of a country's workforce are major factors in determining how well the country's economy will perform. The more highly trained workers are, the higher wages they can command and therefore the more they can consume.

Let us take a closer look at the example of China, mentioned in the example. Their growth has seen the graduate population exploding from 12.3 million in 2000 to 34.6 million in 2013, thus making China an exceptional example of increasing access for students to higher education, according to William Morgan and Bin Wu (2011) of the China Policy Institute, University of Nottingham. One should note that although the rewards are incontestable, the consequences of this exponential growth, according to Morgan and Wu, is that the supply of graduates is likely to exceed labour market demand. However, Jamaica need not worry about this consequence at this time, given that less than 30 per cent of its workforce is tertiary trained. In countries which as at 2019 were experiencing sustained economic growth, the percentage of their workforce which is tertiary trained is in excess of 50 per cent.

Wei Chi, Richard Freeman and Hongbin Li (2015), in an article entitled "Education Attainment and the Labour Market in China, 1989–2013", assure that China's labour market has shown amazing flexibility in responding to the changes in the demand and supply factors of graduates. This they attribute in part to the continued rapid growth of China's economy and a high rate of employee turnover.

Presently, the Jamaican education system is not one which promotes creativity, self-reliance, collaboration and the value of owning one's business. Higher education is an elixir for economic growth and must answer the concerns of survival of higher education graduates. One big concern that Jamaicans and higher education graduates have is that there are not enough jobs for university graduates. All stakeholders must cultivate the resolve to ensure that graduates receive the required skills and competencies while in training to equip them to create their own jobs, locally or abroad, if upon graduating none is available.

The evidence of the relationship between economic development and the education system of a country is irrefutable. The question which citizens, academics, activists and persons who offer themselves for public office must ask is why is it that in Jamaica there seems to be a reticence to invest in education to the extent required. It is often argued, by those who would seek to defend the lack of investment in education, that the country cannot afford to equip schools, pay teachers and fund tertiary education to the degree necessary, as the country is unable to afford it. In addition to the sources of and approaches to funding discussed in chapter 2, the point must be made that if the government has the will, it will find ways of doing what is necessary to fund the education sector to the degree required. The alternative question, however, is: "Can we afford not to fund education to the degree required?" The fact is that the desired goal of sustainable and substantial economic growth and development will not be realized unless there is a radical revision in the level of funding to education.

5.

The Anatomy of Crime
A Jamaican Case Study

As discussed in the previous chapter, crime represents one of the major obstacles to sustained economic growth and development in Jamaica. This chapter explores the anatomy of crime in Jamaica, which has parallels in other Caribbean countries, and offers recommendations for dealing with this pervasive disease. Crime is manifested in many forms in Jamaica, including lotto scamming, fraud, car theft rings, murders, extortion and corruption. Violent crimes, particularly murder, represent the most visible of Jamaica's crime problem, with a rate of 57 murder per 100,000 members of the population, as reported by the 2018 world rankings, which place Jamaica as the second most violent country in the Caribbean, as shown in table 5.1.

In order to portray the profile of what crime, especially murder, looked like in the early stages of post-independence Jamaica, I draw attention to the perspectives of Ellington (2019), a former commissioner of police in Jamaica, who notes that in 1962, the year when Jamaica attained political independence, the murder rate was 3.9 per 100,000, fewer than 100 murders. When a murder occurred, given the limited radio and television penetration levels, people would gather at shops and bars and at neighbours' homes to listen to the account of this rare occurrence. This figure of 3.9 per 100,000 was below the global average of 6 per 100,000. Thus, murder was not always at this high rate. However, in ten years, by 1972, the rate had almost doubled. These murders, though, were largely the result of family feuds and other interpersonal disputes. By 1980, the country recorded over eight hundred murders, mostly related to the political violence which had erupted between the ruling People's National Party and the opposition Jamaica Labour Party in the quest for control of the state.

Crime in Jamaica, particularly murder, has deteriorated and has been described by Bunting (2013), a former minister of national security, and Harriott et al. (2013) a criminologist, as a national security and public health and safety threat. A similar view has been expressed by Williams (2015), a former commissioner of police and criminologist. But according to Levy, a violence prevention activist and sociologist, and Gayle, a criminologist, the problem of crime and violence is largely a public health and community problem and therefore its management must be approached in the same way a public health epidemic is managed. Levy and Gayle shared their perspectives in a report on the the National Crime and Violence Prevention Summit titled "Securing a Safer Jamaica" (Stewart 2019).

The most comprehensive analyses of violence as a public health disease have been argued by Slutkin (2013), who studied violence in Chicago in the United States and other high-crime areas around the world, and also Ward, Lyew Ayee and Ashley (2012), who studied the patterns of violence in Kingston, Jamaica. Slutkin (2013) and Ward et al. (2012) describe violence as a contagious disease and make the assertion that diseases and violence have been responsible for most of the mass fatalities in human history. They also remark that prior to the period when diseases such as leprosy, typhus, cholera and other such diseases were understood as epidemics, those affected by them were blamed for being affected. In a similar way, societies have tended to blame victims of violence for having been victimized. Slutkin makes the further point that the worst decisions that medical practitioners, public health officials and policymakers can make in relation to diseases affecting individuals or society is that of misdiagnosing the cause of the condition.

With violence, and particularly murder, being such a negative psychological and social crisis, the country needs to deepen its understanding of root causes to arrive at appropriate solutions to anatomize it. Slutkin provides some useful insights to this end, from which Jamaica can learn. He asserts that violence is a phenomenon driven by the brain and argues that if that and other scientific findings about human behaviour are connected with what is known from infectious disease epidemiology, a new set of causations and strategies to reduce violence can be created more predictably. He concludes that containing violence requires both an understanding of how the brain processes violent experiences and the epidemiology of diseases. With respect to the latter, Slutkin itemizes the three critical variables in the management of infectious diseases in populations, namely clustering, spread and transmission. Therefore, translated to the context of crime, Jamaican crime fighters and policymakers need to isolate and cluster the different forms and types of murders, determine what motivates each and implement strategies to prevent widespread occurrence or even to totally obliterate it.

Ward et al. (2012) also posit some useful insights into the anatomy of violence, which find applicability to the murder situation in Jamaica. They conclude that it seems likely that the stress of violence in the community finds expression in violence in the home. In turn, it is also likely that children who experience violence in the home more often than not grow up into young adults who perpetrate violence in the community. This view is corroborated by Slutkin, who explains that clustering in space, or spatial grouping, provides the ideal condition for the rapid spread of diseases but the spread is not linear, which is why many researchers will have difficulty attributing rises and falls to simple causative factors. Once there is clustering, there will be transmission asymmetrically and a rapid spread. The key then to limiting transmission is to identify those who have been affected and quarantine them from the rest of the population until they are cured or until the acuity of the condition has been minimized to prevent transmission.

The positions advanced by Gayle (as he shared the academic/anthropological perspective at the National Crime and Violence Prevention Summit held in July 2019), Harriott et al. (2013), Levy (2019) and Williams (2015) that the disease model for dealing with the culture of violence in Jamaica is the most effective and the most sustainable should find agreement with policymakers and crime fighters.

Locating Jamaica's Crime Statistics Regionally and Historically

Jamaica's crime rate, which had reached as high as 62 per 100,000 in 2009, stood at about 40 per 100,000 in 2018, making Jamaica the sixth most violent place on the planet, as shown in table 5.1. The murder rate is greater than regions of the world which are experiencing civil war.

Table 5.1. Caribbean and Latin American Countries on the Ranking of Twenty-Five Countries with the Highest Rates of Murder per Capita (2018)

#	Country	Region	Ranking	Murder Rate per 100,000 Population
1	Honduras	Latin America	1	90.4
2	Venezuela	Latin America	2	53.7
3	Belize	Caribbean	3	44.7
4	El Salvador	Latin America	4	41.2
5	Guatemala	Latin America	5	39.9
6	Jamaica	Caribbean	6	39.3
7	St. Kitts and Nevis	Caribbean	9	33.6
8	Colombia	Latin American	11	30.8
9	Bahamas	Caribbean	12	29.8
10	Trinidad and Tobago	Caribbean	13	28.3

(Continued)

Table 5.1. (*continued*)

#	Country	Region	Ranking	Murder Rate per 100,000 Population
11	St Vincent and the Grenadines	Caribbean	15	25.6
12	Brazil	Latin America	16	25.2
13	Dominica Republic	Caribbean	18	22.1
14	St Lucia	Caribbean	19	21.6
15	Mexico	Latin America	20	21.5
16	Dominica	Caribbean	21	21.1
17	Panama	Latin America	25	17.2

Murders in Jamaica: Gangs and Guns

As noted in the discussion on the anatomy of crime, most murders which occurred in Jamaica prior to 1980 were attributable to domestic disputes, with the main weapons being knives and machetes. Political violence was responsible for most murders in 1980 and into the 1990s. However, since the mid-1990s rival gangs have been responsible for most of the murders. Since at least 2009, 80 per cent of murders have been committed using the gun, and most involving gangs. This is according to Ellington (2019), who traced the evolution of gangs across four generations. But what is responsible for this manifestation of crime? The answer is that the gun trade, which is controlled by gangs, is responsible for the high rate of gang- and gun-related murders in Jamaica. While the gun has been the weapon of choice in murders in Jamaica, moving from 69.9 per cent in 2012 to 74 per cent in 2013 and 80 per cent since 2016, the gun is symptomatic of, rather than the root cause of, crime.

The United States has the most guns, at 112.6 guns per 100 residents, and while having a high rate of gun crime, the United States does not figure in the top ten nations with the highest rates of murder. Honduras, which tops the list of the most violent countries in the world, has a gun-related murder rate of 67.18 per 100,000 residents, compared to Jamaica in fifth position at 30.72 gun-related murders per 100,000 residents, according to data from the Small Arms Survey. Thus, if guns were the root cause of crime, then the United States should be in the top ten. Instead, consider the assertion that the prevalence of gangs is the proximate underlying cause of the high rates of murders in Jamaica and that the ultimate underlying causes are the socio-economic and political conditions which produce those gangs.

Ellington (2019), in his analysis of the generations of gangs, suggests that "first-generation" gangs are loosely structured itinerant groups of youths involved in robberies and who provide services to their "second-generation" counterparts. The second-generation gangs exhibit some form of structure and are involved in criminal businesses. A major feature of these gangs is their fight for the control of certain areas which represent the base of their illicit activities, including extortion. Third-generation gangs are well organized and operate legitimate businesses and as part of their attempts to legitimize themselves, they get involved in social investments. Fourth-generation gangs consist of individuals who have been co-opted as sympathizers and facilitators of organized crime.

The criminal gangs which operate in Jamaica are predominantly found in four main parishes, namely the western parishes of St James and Westmoreland and the eastern parishes of St Catherine, Kingston and St Andrew. In 2018, following an exceedingly murderous year in Jamaica when 1,641 persons were murdered, with St James accounting for about 20 per cent of that number, the then government declared a state of emergency in that parish. During that same year, states of emergency were also declared in southern St Andrew and northern St Catherine. After a brief suspension of the states of emergency in those parishes, another one was declared in April 2019, and on that occasion the one in western Jamaica included Westmoreland and Hanover, along with St James, in addition to northern St Catherine and southern St Andrew.

What was striking is that while the states of emergency were in operation, as would be expected, murders were on the decline, but as soon as they were suspended, murders began to trend upwards. Data from the Jamaica Constabulary Force for July 2019 show that in St James, for example, data from the total number of murders in the first seven months of 2018 during the state of emergency, was fifty-six, but in the corresponding period of 2019 the total number was seventy-nine, a 41.1 per cent increase with a state of emergency in place in the last three months of that period. A similar, but less dramatic, situation occurred in the policing division of southern St Andrew, with a 12.8 per cent increase in murders in 2019 over 2018 following the removal of the state of emergency in 2019. What the data suggest is that crime is out of control despite multiple security measures. It is my contention, however, that the problem posed by criminal gangs cannot be solved with tough policing measures; they must be solved by radically reforming the education system and giving stronger social support to families such that more children go to, stay in and do well in school.

Gayle (in Stewart 2019) analyses the pattern of murders pre- and post-strong policing interventions and found that, as expected, there is a decline in criminal activities when interventions are implemented, but found that in some cases, the post-intervention period shows higher levels of criminal activity than the pre-intervention period. Gayle's conclusion is that tough policing measures are not sustainable in reducing crime. He proposes a more inclusive set of solutions which consider the sociological factors that lead youths to get involved in crime. Phillips (in Stewart 2019), in highlighting that Jamaica recorded about 13,000 murders over the ten-year period from 2009 to 2018, notes that there are between 160,000 and 175,000 unattached youth in Jamaica and that with about three hundred gangs operating in the country, these tens of thousands of youths are easy conscripts for engagement in criminal activities. Thus, he, too, a former minister of national security, argues that tough policing measures are not the most appropriate response to the wave of crime and murders, as these tough measures do not address root causes.

With the large cohort of unattached youth, the primary strategy must be reducing the rate at which other youths are being added to that constituency of persons, and this means providing support to families and strengthening the education system.

Getting to the Root Causes: Social Conditions which Produce Gangs

Data from the Jamaica Constabulary Force indicate, and Ellington (2019) confirms, that most of the murders committed in Jamaica are carried out by gangs or gang members and that 70 to 80 per cent of them are gang related. These are not domestic crimes or crimes targeting women and children per se. If that were so, one would expect that a significant amount of the government's attention would be devoted to dealing with gangs. In early 2017, within a matter of a few weeks, the police and the military took out about ten high-profile suspects, six of whom were taken down one night in St James, as reported by the *Gleaner* in January 2017. Their neutralization did not make a dent in the high levels of murders taking place in St James, and 2017 turned out to be the bloodiest year ever in terms of murders in a single parish in Jamaica, with 341 murders representing 21 per cent of the 1,608 murders in Jamaica that year. It was this record number of murders in 2017, which represented an increase of nearly 20 per cent over the 1,350 murders recorded in 2016.

These facts support the case that Ellington (2019) makes that the strategy of tough policing as a tool to reduce murders is not effective. The cure lies in dealing with the root causes of what produces gangs and thus devoting the resources for treating the same. Devoting resources for dealing with gangs cannot mean boots and bullets. On the contrary, while some amount of force might be necessary to repel armed gangs, the sustainable treatment of gangs and the gang culture means getting to the root cause. The root causes of gang culture in Jamaica are the socio-economic and sociopolitical conditions under which underprivileged, mainly black, youth grow up and live.

Erica Allen, a social worker with the Peace Management Initiative, discusses the experience of that organization in dealing with crime in one of the most violence-prone and violence-affected communities of St Catherine. Sharing the violence interrupter perspective, Allen (in Stewart 2019) notes that for the three-year period 2016–18, homicide results ranged from 100 per cent reduction in Lakes Pen, to 88 per cent at St John's Road, to 76 per cent in March Pen. These levels of reduction were not the result of policing interventions, however, but the result of teaching conflict management skills, supporting youths in schools, teaching parenting, facilitating inter-group and inter-community engagements and providing personal and educational development opportunities and employment.

Citing some characteristics of the at-risk youths who are targeted by the Peace Management Initiative, Allen provides some data on these youths, noting the following:

- 60 per cent of them were incarcerated at least once
- 78 per cent of them dropped out of school
- 60 per cent grew up in a single-parent household
- 80 per cent of them dropped out of school because of a lack of money
- 80 per cent had a family member killed
- 70 per cent were involved in gang activity

As already noted, heavy policing is not the cure for dealing with the realities mentioned here, which are common across many of Jamaica's inner-city communities. Levy (2019) makes this case compellingly, highlighting other communities in which there have been drastic reductions in the incidence of violence as a result of measures other than "tough" policing, specifically states of emergency. The communities Levy cites which have experienced significant reductions in crime are among those in the northern St Catherine police division, previously one of the most violent areas of Jamaica, which was under a state of emergency during periods in 2018 and 2019. These communities include De La Vega City, Jones Pen, Job Lane and Tawes Pen. Levy notes that for the three months from February to April 2019, since the ending of the state of emergency, the ten communities in the division recorded only two shootings and three homicides. Levy attributes this phenomenal achievement to the work being done by violence interrupters and community builders of the Peace Management Initiative working alongside community-based police.

Interrupting violence represents the first dimension of the application of the disease control model of managing crime and violence, as proposed by Slutkin (2013), Gayle (in Stewart 2019) and Levy (2019). In the absence of these social interventions, the violence experienced by these youth will become endemic and spread rapidly. The application of the disease model means first isolating the affected youths. During isolation they will be facilitated in talking through their exposure to the disease, come to terms with its effects on them and enabled to find paths to excise those effects. These paths will include opportunities for meaningful occupation, education, training and exposure to lifestyles and life situations that are different from those out of which they have come. In practical terms, this isolation means creating specially defined zones within or outside the communities which are designed to re-socialize the youths. This process of re-socialization would involve (1) learning to live peacefully with others; (2) acquiring marketable skills; (3) developing personal self-discipline; and (4) embracing new values which promote communal and national development.

These specially created zones could be training camps outside the diseased communities or a flooding of the actual diseased community with the required resources. These training camps or the newly resourced community would be equipped with the resources to deliver the four elements of the re-socialization agenda. While the strategies of isolating affected youth are being implemented, resources will also be devoted to altering the socio-economic conditions which created the communities in the first place. This means that government will invest in improving the resources available to schools, including paying teachers who work in these communities more attractive salaries; supporting the creation of productive enterprises; providing support to families at the margins; and nurturing a culture of lawfulness, social cohesion and the transmission of value systems which advance the foregoing.

It is the combination of the strategies of isolation of the affected youths and exposing them to alternative lifestyles, while treating with the problems and conditions plaguing their communities of origin, which would result in the contained spread of the disease. The rapid spread of violence across Jamaica and the exponential increase in the murder rate since 1972 may thus be attributable to a faulty diagnosis of causation and consequently the application of the wrong treatment. Despite the high murder rate now being experienced in Jamaica, it can still go higher until treated appropriately. But as Slutkin (2013) notes, the spread of diseases is non-linear and causation is multifold. I will, therefore, now turn attention to some of the other causes of crime.

Getting to Root Causes: At-Risk and Unattached Youth

Heywood and Lawrence (2014) discuss the problem of unattached youth and highlight the fact that they represent a major source into which criminal gangs tap for new recruits. Thus, a major phenomenon which serves to perpetuate the high crime rate in Jamaica is the legions of youth who have dropped out of school. Although having "completed" high school, they are unqualified for low-level jobs or vocational or tertiary education, and in some cases even though they may qualify, are not interested. The Human Employment and Resource Training Trust (HEART/NTA 2009) defines unattached youth as those who are in the age group of fourteen to twenty-four years, unemployed or outside the labour force and not in school or in training. As stated elsewhere in this chapter, it is estimated that there are between 160,000 and 175,000 unattached youths in Jamaica. With this large number and given the nearly three hundred gangs operating in Jamaica, as noted by Phillips at the National Crime and Violence Prevention Summit in 2019, what the state must consider is the required scale of social intervention that would be needed to cauterize the problem of youths freely flowing into criminal gangs.

In 2015 the government at the time introduced the National Unattached Youth Programme, which offered a stipend, remedial education, skills training and apprenticeships to youths aged seventeen to thirty who were not in a job or studying. The programme was short-lived, and as of early 2016, a total of 3,877 youths across the island were registered in it. Concerns have been expressed by violence reduction experts about the apparent lack of coordination between and among various social intervention initiatives. This lack of coordination has been deemed responsible for the failures of some of these programmes (Gayle in Stewart 2019). One could also consider whether the collective will has the required level of commitment to make these programmes effective.

In early 2017, the Jamaica Defence Force announced that it would be setting up two bases in western Jamaica and in addition introduced a new recruitment drive called the National Service Enlistment. This enlistment initiative would be implemented alongside a government initiative called Learning, Earning, Giving Back and Saving (LEGS). According to Major Basil Jarrett, who was quoted in the *Sunday Observer* of 12 March 2017, the National Service Enlistment would train approximately one thousand people aged eighteen to twenty-three over a one-year period in military, vocational, and broader life skills. There was also a report that the Ministry of Education had plans to introduce life skills, under the Career Advancement Programme, in twenty schools.

The National Service Enlistment and LEGS (while not new in content and focus) represent an attempt to address root causes of crime, but with such a large cohort of unattached youth, the government will have to spend massive amounts of money to correct the problems they have produced over the years. In other words, the token numbers of youths being recruited and trained by the Jamaica Defence Force, which is about one thousand each year, is almost infinitesimal when compared to the size of the problem which exists. At such a low rate of targeting unattached youth, it means that the vast majority will never be reached. It therefore means that the investment in responding to the needs of unattached youth will have to be increased exponentially.

While the state must lead the way in combatting the problem of crime and violence, and in doing so to help reduce the large number of youths who are available as easy conscripts for gangs, other groups in society must play a role. In this regard, an initiative announced by the Adventist Church in 2017 to invest in the training of seven thousand youth, is a most commendable gesture. The initiative of the Adventists, like that being undertaken by other churches and non-governmental organizations, confirms what has long been known: that fighting crime requires the input of the entire community.

Getting to the Root Causes: Gangs and Political Parties

The 2011 Anti-Gang Strategy of the Jamaica Constabulary Force showed that at least two hundred criminal gangs were operating in Jamaica. By 2019, the police estimate put the number of gangs operating in Jamaica at near three hundred. Many of these gangs identify themselves with either the People's National Party or the Jamaica Labour Party. Since the early 2000s the two most notorious gangs in Jamaica have been the One Order Gang and the Clansman Gang. Other well-known gangs are the Stone Crusher, Presidential Click, Matthews Lane and East Kingston gangs. Each of these have had declared or strongly suspected or plausibly established political affiliations or sympathies, and the members of some of these gangs have received varying levels of tacit or explicit support from political leaders on both sides of the political divide. There have been several news reports of incidents in which political leaders, including elected officials, have come to the aid of or used state resources to support or defend members of known gangs or known gang leaders. Williams and Roth (2011) argue, citing White (1967) and Clarke (2006), that the Jamaica Labour Party and People's National Party are actively engaged with gangs, having recruited them as enforcers in the political warfare. Former prime minister Bruce Golding openly admitted in 1993 that he was associated with gunmen (meaning members of gangs) and made this assertion in seeking to dispassionately describe the relationship between politicians and gangs in Jamaica. While Golding was making a personal declaration of sorts, he was quick to explain that he was not unique.

It is thus fair to say that one of the root causes of gangs and the gang culture has been the tacit or explicit support which governmental officials have afforded them. It has not helped that the expected expression of public repudiation and disassociation supported by policies and public actions to cripple gangs, which the public expects of political leaders, has not been seen. If we look at the locations that have been at the centre of much of the criminality in Jamaica over several decades, it would not be difficult to see the validity of the long-held view articulated by Gayle (in Stewart 2019) and Levy (2019) that there is a link between politics and crime. That most gangs exist in political strongholds and most murders are committed by persons in political strongholds would appear to suggest that in order to reduce murders and crime generally, these garrisons must be eliminated.

This suggestion that government should take steps towards eliminating garrisons was echoed as one of the recommendations of the David Simmonds Tivoli Commission of Inquiry report of 2011. The data provided by the Jamaica Constabulary Force which show that 70 to 80 per cent of murders are committed by gangs have not been refuted. It is therefore a valid argument that the factors that produce criminal gangs are the root cause of crime. The suggestion or evidence that political parties, whether in government or in their role as opposition, have been associated with gangsters makes it an urgent need for any nexus that may exist to be repudiated by policy action and practice.

There is a lethal combination among three factors which breed crime, namely unattached youth, criminal gangs and alliances of gangs to political parties. Members of a political party wishing to retain or gain a stronghold on a political constituency will likely not see the dispersal of youth into gainful activity, which makes them indifferent to and independent of the political system, as a good thing. In stark political terms it would be antithetical to the retaining of the powerbase of a political stronghold for "at-risk" youth to be diverted from becoming gang members. It thus appears to be the case that the maintenance of political strongholds depends on having youths become members of gangs, as they are ready to be or already are foot soldiers for the control of political turfs. It is a moot point as to whether many politicians really want it to be any other way. This point is strongly implied in the 2011 Anti-Gang Strategy.

Another insight that may be gleaned from the Anti-Gang strategy is how patently conflicted governments are in dealing with crime. On the one hand, it has been known for a long time that there is a strong relationship between political strongholds and crime, including and especially murders, yet our political representatives vote to spend billions of dollars to deal with the symptoms, rather than the root causes, whereas by many of their actions, some continue to contribute to the existence of crime. It is to be noted that the development of the Anti-Gang Strategy was funded with assistance from bilateral trading partners and donor agencies. If our political leaders and government were to have the courage to take on the root causes of crime, large swaths of funds would be available to fund sustainable diversion programmes involving "at-risk" youth.

The convenient relationship among the factors of crime, unattached youth and political strongholds was in evidence in the furore over a court order issued in October 2016 requiring that several illegal occupants who were squatting on a property at 85 Red Hills Road be removed. In response to the court order, member of Parliament Karl Samuda criticized the court for making what he described as a foolish decision. The *Gleaner* newspaper, in a story carried on 25 December 2016, reported that Samuda came in for heavy criticism from several sectors of the society, including the Bar Association and the opposition. The consensus among these critics was that the comments of the member of Parliament were highly inappropriate, and some demanded he apologize for attacking judges in that manner. Samuda reportedly said he would not. Instead, he vowed that he would use the provisions of the Local Improvements (Communities Amenities) Act 1977 to forcibly acquire the land – a decision the government later implemented.

The acquisition of the named property by the government may be seen through several lenses, one of which is that the location housed dozens of diehard supporters of the member of Parliament of the ruling party. The removal of these persons would mean fewer guaranteed votes, and thus it is a convenient arrangement to have large numbers of political supporters move into legally or illegally occupied property. Squatting not only represents a blight on the environment and disregard for property rights but also a breeding bed for criminals. The use of the law to legitimize squatter settlements which provide cash for votes, in addition to providing a cover for the flourishing of criminality, represents a form of tacit endorsement of lawlessness, which should not forsake reproach. The utterances and actions of the government are likely to embolden others to engage in the practice. Many of the hotbeds of crime in the four major crime-producing parishes of Kingston and St Andrew, Clarendon, St Catherine and St James have massive squatter settlements, some of which have been legitimized by the state. These communities include areas in and around Spanish Town, May Pen, Tucker, Red Hills Road, Flanker, Granville, Norwood and West Kingston, among others.

Gangs and guns often go hand in hand with drugs, as well as other criminal activities such as extortion and contract killings. Williams (2007) notes that the problem of gangs, guns and drugs in Jamaican society is exacerbated by the fact that Jamaica is a transit zone for drugs headed to North America from Latin America. According to Williams (2007), Jamaica's precarious position is characterized by several unhelpful variables. Some of these include proximity to both the major producers and consumers of illicit drugs, its vulnerable entry points, porosity of borders, the presence of local organized criminal networks, weak political structures and inadequate law enforcement infrastructure. None of the two possible outcomes of the foregoing is desirable. In one instant, the gangs have access to resources which make them more lethal and independent of the political machinery. At the same time they are so equipped and resourced that they can be more useful and effective in supporting the political party of their choice.

The combination of gangs, guns, drugs, corrupt politicians and police personnel thus becomes a major national security threat, and if the obstacles posed by crime to the sustainable development of Jamaica are to be overcome, there must be political will on the part of politicians to fully disassociate themselves and their political parties from gangs. There also has to be a corresponding commitment to deal with the problem of source reduction, which means improving the education system.

Getting at Root the Causes: Re-export of Gangs from the United States

Williams and Roth (2011) examined the rise and fall of Jamaican gangs operating in the United States and found that while the Jamaican gangs, which were dominant in the inner cities of Kingston became well known in the United States during the 1980s and 1990s, they have virtually disappeared from the American landscape. Their disappearance from the streets of the United States, as a result of aggressive US anti-drug and anti-gang operations and immigration policies, has resulted in their displacement or relocation to Jamaica. Among them were the two largest and most influential gangs in Jamaica: the Tivoli Gardens and the Matthews Lane gangs, which were loyal to the Jamaica Labour Party and People's National Party, respectively, and were known in the United States as the Shower Posse and the Spranglers Posse, according to the US Department of Justice (1990).

The theory which underlies the aggressive immigration policies, which resulted in the displacement of gang members from the United States, may be referred to as the importation theory or the urban conspiracy theory (Ubah 2007). This theory posits that gang violence in the United States is a product of pre-entry to the United States and pre-incarceration cultures of inmates. Thus, to curb the problem, the solution lies in deporting persons associated with gangs even if they had grown up in the United States. The problem this has presented for Jamaican law enforcement is that many of these deported persons become agents for their gang members remaining in the United States, as well as in the United Kingdom. In their role as agents, these gangsters are involved in drug trafficking and importation of guns and ammunition and thus pose a major challenge to law enforcement (Williams 2015).

The solution to this problem of displaced gangsters is complex, but fundamentally rests in the application of the disease control model. In applying this model, the state will be required to identify and isolate these former gang members and treat them. Treatment possibilities could include but are not limited to providing re-socialization interventions, as well as alternative economic opportunities. Additionally, the state would have need to insulate the contexts out of which they operate. It can achieve this by ensuring that youths in those communities have access to proper education and training, as well as meaningful employment and continued acculturation in the norms and values which are deemed helpful to promote social transformation through sustainable community development.

Getting to the Root Causes: Weak Family Structures

Weak family systems are major contributors to the early entry of youths, especially boys, into a life of crime. Thus, part of the solution to the problem of unattached youth is to be found in providing greater support for families with limited financial, social and parental resources. In addition there is the problem of abusive parents, many of whom were themselves abused as children.

Gayle (in Stewart 2019) points to abusive mother–son relationships as a major contributor to crime and violence. Gayle found that abused boys account for 53 per cent of murders in Jamaica and thus cautions that in order to interrupt the cycle of violence in Jamaica, attention needs to be paid to enabling mothers to be better at parenting. While not discounting the important role fathers play in the life of boys, Gayle points out that Jamaica now has the highest number of fathers in 2019 in its households, with 42 per cent of households having both a mother and a father. This rate is higher than at any other point in Jamaica's history, yet murders have continued to climb. The percentage of households in which both parents were present seventy years earlier, in 1948, was 18 per cent, yet that was one of the most peaceful periods in Jamaica's post-slavery history.

Gayle observes that the increase in households where fathers are present runs parallel to the annual increases in murders since independence, with 2017 recording the third-highest number of murders in the country's history. Gayle comments further on the 53 per cent of murders being perpetrated by abused boys, adding that the same figure of 53 per cent is involved in repeat killings and thus concludes that most murders are committed by abused and traumatized boys who are also repeat killers. Gayle's findings require further scrutiny. One area which needs elucidation, for example, is whether the drivers of the abusive behaviours of these mothers could relate to the absence of a father or other forms of family support. What has also not been established is whether those mothers were themselves abused. So, while there may be a relationship between abusive mothers and boys who commit murders, the cause of the propensity to murder cannot be established based on these facts.

Coombs (2018) contends that the absence of fathers is a major contributor to the scale of crime and violence in Jamaica. Coombs takes issue with Gayle, who had espoused the view questioning the assertion that there is a relationship between absent fathers and boys getting involved in crime. Gayle, who reiterated his position in 2019, was not, however, suggesting that the presence of fathers would not make a difference in boys' involvement in crime; rather, Gayle's argument is that the parenting styles of mothers is a major contributor.

Coombs's position is supported by Kruk (2012), who cites a 2007 United Nations Children Fund study which found, among other things, that fatherless children have more difficulties with social adjustment. The study shows that 71 per cent of high school dropouts are fatherless and that they are more likely to leave school at age sixteen and less likely to attain academic and professional qualifications in adulthood. Most critically in relation to crime, the study found that 85 per cent of youth in prison have an absent father. Ward et al. (2012) explore the impact of trauma on children and suggest that interventions such as training in life skills such as self-esteem and conflict management can interrupt the cycle of violence and reduce the rage so often seen in violent acts.

The question which remains then is what types of intervention programmes exist to help these traumatized children who are vulnerable to violent tendencies. Ward et al. (2012.) mention some intervention programmes which appear to have had some success in reducing violence in Jamaica. These include Children First, the Child Abuse Mitigation Project and the Child Resiliency Programme. Children First, Ward et al. note, has been recognized internationally for its creative and participatory approach. The programme has been used in schools, mental health services, churches, local businesses and community organizations targeting high-risk adolescents. The evaluations of the programme show reductions in fights and violence-related injuries, along with better school attendance and better grades. Another initiative, the Child Abuse Mitigation Project, is located at the Bustamante Hospital for Children and developed a model to identify and refer victims of violence, while the Child Resiliency Programme provides counselling. Ward et al. note that while these initiatives have not all undergone rigorous evaluation, the results suggest that they have had a positive impact on the participants.

The perspectives of Gayle (in Stewart 2019), Kruk (2012) and Ward et al. (2012) all point to the critical importance of providing support to vulnerable families as a means of reducing exposure to violence and helping families manage (meaning cope with and recover from) the challenges associated with structural and environmental deficiencies in life arising from crime and violence.

Zones of Special Operation

The Government of Jamaica has from time to time responded to the need to curb crime by implementing several crime fighting strategies. As the scourge of crime is persistent, so are the efforts of successive governments to scramble to find solutions. The most recent in a line of initiatives established by the Government of Jamaica is the law named Zones of Special Operations. Under this law, the government may declare a geographical area a special zone and in addition to increasing police and military presence, expand the availability of social services in the area. These social services include assistance in obtaining birth certificates, tax registration numbers, and registration in vocational training programmes. The strategy as conceived and articulated in terms of the measures of success enunciated by the government was designed to reduce crime, especially murders. Like the others, the Zones of Special Operations is not without its challenges, but much can be done to ensure their success, if the government undertakes certain measures.

The high crime rate in Jamaica is not the doing of any one political party. The high crime rate is Jamaica's problem, and unless a bipartisan, non-politicized approach is taken, we run the risk of infusing political one-upmanship in initiatives that could end up undermining the efforts towards real crime reduction. The crime fighting platform should not be one from which players seek to become great or obtain applause. Rather, the focus must be on outcomes. If there is a governing principle of indifference to being seen as great, then the capacity for collaboration increases and results yielded become more achievable. It is here that the engagement in a bipartisan approach becomes possible.

Information on conditions and community characteristics that must be the subject of transformation activities should therefore be at the forefront of the discussions about the Zones of Special Operations, not largely getting illegal guns and capturing criminals. Getting illegal guns and capturing criminals is everyday police work. Assured that money will be available to support a massive and sustained intervention, the Social Intervention Committee must then put together a master plan for dealing with the root causes of crime.

Conclusions and Recommendations

Given what has been established about the relationship between unattached youth and violent crimes and unemployment and involvement in crime, the focus of strategic crime fighting efforts must be as follows:

1. The provision of funding for and greater monitoring of the various programmes that target unattached youth, including the Career Advancement Programme
2. The resumption or remodelling of the National Unattached Youth Programme and the defining of a clear articulation with LEGS
3. The passing of legislation that will make it mandatory for unattached and unemployed youth under the age of eighteen years to be attached to a programme of education and skill training, including greater investment in children's homes and places of safety and for street children under age eighteen to be automatically removed from the streets to places of safety
4. Increasing investment to reduce teenage pregnancy and among those who are unable to provide for children they produce
5. Strengthening of parenting support systems
6. The continued strengthening of an institutional working relationship between the Jamaica Defence Force and the soon-to-be merged entity comprising the Human Employment and Resource Training Trust/ National Training Agency, the National Youth Service and the Jamaica Foundation for Lifelong Learning
7. Increasing investment in and non-partisan spending on social infrastructure (with strict compliance with the procurement guidelines) to create employment opportunities and increase economic activity
8. More effective targeting of the intended beneficiaries of the Career Advancement Programme to cater to a wider cross-section of school dropouts with a focus on a broader range of life skills

Part 3

Leadership and Institutional Development

6.

Leadership Development
Caribbean Political Leadership in the Spotlight

Caribbean political leadership in the current era has retreated somewhat from the strong global presence which it held in the latter half of the twentieth century, particularly during the era of the 1950s to the 1980s. During that period Caribbean leadership was inspirational and visionary. Many of the leaders of their respective countries were the founders of nation-states or those who immediately succeeded them, and they collectively displayed a strong belief in exemplary leadership. Three of these leaders – Errol Barrow of Barbados, Norman Manley of Jamaica and Eric Williams of Trinidad and Tobago – were mentioned in the preface but to that list could be added many others not only from the political arena but also in academia, business, culture and sports. Among the pieces of evidence which exist to support the view that in the late twentieth century Caribbean leaders across several spheres were looked to provide guidance, direction, inspiration and vision are the levels of voter turnout in general elections. This, among other relevant issues, will be the subject of discussion in this chapter.

While the regional and global contexts within which the founders of Caribbean nation-states operated may have changed, and while those who immediately succeeded them continue to make the presence of the region felt in global circles, whether the non-aligned movement; the Africa, Caribbean and Pacific network; academic influence; or sporting dominance, the profile of the region on the global stage is markedly different in the twenty-first century than it was in the twentieth century. Yet the duty of leaders remains largely the same in every generation – that of providing guidance, direction and inspiration to those they lead (Burns 1978; Maxwell 1998; Posner and Kouzes 1988). The duty of leaders is to inspire the better angels in us, and leaders cannot inspire others unless they are able to communicate a vision (Heatherfield 2018).

Consequently, Caribbean societies are at a crossroads with respect to how we will define ourselves as a region over the course of the next several generations. Bernal (2019) highlights one of the major issues at this crossroads, namely the role of China in the economic development of the region. The second is the emergence of right-wing extremism which is dominating global politics and challenging the status quo in Europe, the United Kingdom and the United States. While the political temperature in the Caribbean has been fairly stable over the last twenty years, it is not improbable that the presence of China could trigger geo-political rivalry and serious tensions with the United States and later lead to reactionary political fervour, which could be exploited by right-wing extremists.

The prospect of right-wing extremism emerging in the Caribbean is related not only to the global trend of right-wing political "revolts", as seen in Brexit and the rise of the right in Europe (Galston 2018) but also relates to the fact that for the better part of the period of its political independence, Caribbean countries have been led by politicians who have been more akin to left-wing or left-of-centre political tendencies. This has been the case not only in the Barbados (under Errol Barrow and Tom Adams), Jamaica (under Norman Manley and Michael Manley) and Trinidad and Tobago (under Eric Williams), as discussed earlier, but also in Antigua and Barbuda under Vere Bird and his son Lester, the Bahamas under Lyndon Pindling and Guyana under Cheddie Jagan and Forbes Burnham.

Thus, one of the major issues which Caribbean countries will be required to determine in the next decade will be their respective political philosophies and ideological leanings in a political era in which China, rather than the United Kingdom or the United States, is the dominant global power.

Voting Patterns as Evidence of Political Interest

One of the primary pieces of evidence of the commitment of citizens to assume collective leadership, and at the same time the strongest indication of apathy, is participation in the political process through voting. Social activism is an advanced form of citizens' leadership and as shown in chapter 3, has been on the decline in the Caribbean. Citizens' leadership in the form of voting has also been on the decline.

Data from the Electoral Commission of Jamaica show that voter turnout in general elections had a mean of 80.51 per cent between 1962 and 1980 across five election cycles, ranging from a low of 72.29 per cent to a high of 86.1 per cent. By contrast, between 1989 and 2016, across seven general elections, voter turnout averaged 61.56 per cent – a difference of approximately nineteen percentage points. (The turnout for 1983 was not included in the analysis, as the opposition did not contest that election.) While there were charges of electoral fraud in some seats, which could alter the turnout figures, there is no doubt that the level of enthusiasm of the general population and the reliance on the leadership of the country for direction was higher in the pre-1989 period versus 1989 and after. An examination of data from the Barbados Election Centre (2018) shows that voter turnout had a mean of 76.74 per cent over five general election cycles, from 1966 (the year the country got its independence) to 1986. Turnout peaked at 81.64 per cent in 1971 and had a low of 71.59 per cent in 1981. By contrast, turnout averaged 61.32 per cent between 1991 and 2018 in seven election cycles, with the highest being 63.36 per cent in 1999 and the lowest 59.41 per cent in 1991. A comparative analysis of the voter turnout in Trinidad and Tobago is somewhat problematic, as data from the Elections and Boundaries Commission of that republic show. With the country being ruled by one prime minister, Eric Williams, for twenty years from 1962 to 1981, the pattern of voter turnout shows that in the 1961 general elections the turnout was 88.1 per cent but fell to 65.8 per cent in 1966. There was a boycott by opposition parties in 1971, but in 1976 the turnout was 55.8 per cent. In the latter era of voting in Trinidad and Tobago, in the 1990s to the early 2000s, the pattern shows a consistent turnout in the mid to high sixties, ranging from a low of 63.3 per cent in 1995 to a high of 69.9 per cent in 2002, closely marked by 69.45 per cent in 2010.

The two main political parties in Trinidad and Tobago also experienced the power of the people to reject what they do not support. In 2015 the incumbent People's Partnership Coalition, which had the United National Congress as the biggest member, was defeated by the Keith Rowley–led People's National Movement. According to a report posted by the Oxford Business Group, the issues around which the contest was framed were crime and corruption and integrity in the public sector. Hutchinson-Jafar (2015) also reported that the campaign had centred on a range of accusations of government corruption. In all three cases cited, the election results were influenced by increased citizen agitation.

The March 2018 general elections in Antigua and Barbuda represent somewhat of an outlier or contrast to the three cases cited earlier. While the party in power was faced with accusations of misconduct, specifically bribery, Prime Minister Gaston Browne had been involved in a public spat with businessman and tourism mogul Gordon "Butch" Stewart in which the latter was deemed to be making unreasonable demands on the government, including tax concessions and write-offs. Stewart was also reported to have threatened to close down his hotels in the country if the government did not acquiesce to his demands. Public commentaries suggested that Stewart was also deemed to be showing disrespect to the office of the prime minister and Browne specifically. The outcomes of the elections were that Browne's Antigua and Barbuda Labour

Party increased its hold on power by winning an additional seat, moving its majority from fourteen to fifteen of seventeen seats.

What readers can draw from the assessment of the results of the Antigua and Barbuda elections is that citizens took umbrage to the alleged display of disrespect by Stewart towards Prime Minister Browne. It is reasonable to conclude that in the minds of the voters, 76.3 per cent of whom turned out to vote, the alleged disrespect shown towards Browne was greater than the wrongdoing of which he was accused. This 76.3 per cent turnout may be viewed from two perspectives. First, when compared to 90.08 per cent turnout in the previous election in 2014, which was also won by Browne's Antigua and Barbuda Labour Party, the decline in turnout may be viewed as a rebuke to Browne in relation to the allegations that were made against him. But second, the massive turnout in 2014 may be viewed as a vote against the United Progressive Party, which had won the 2004 and the 2009 elections. Turnouts in these elections were 91.19 per cent and 80.27 per cent, respectively. But these levels of turnout may be seen as rebuke voting, as in the previous four elections – 1999, 1994, 1989 and 1984 – all of which were won by the Antigua and Barbuda Labour Party (known then as the Antigua Labour Party), turnout showed a mean of 61.93 per cent. Thus, while the 76.03 per cent turnout in 2018 was lower than the immediate past three elections, it was higher than the four preceding ones. A definite message was being sent to business leaders as well, that they, too, are accountable and that a certain level of conduct is demanded of them. Ultimately, then, the parameters for leadership development in the Caribbean are being defined by the decisions of the people.

The foregoing analysis confirms a declining level of interest of citizens in the political process and declining admiration for political leaders. Kirton, Anatol and Braithwaite (2010), in the Latin America Public Opinion Project, conducted a survey in Trinidad and Tobago using a stratified random sample of 1,503 citizens evenly divided between males and females. It found, among other things, that 52 per cent of the population were either dissatisfied or very dissatisfied with democracy in the twin-island state, with 41 per cent being dissatisfied. The study further found that only 2 per cent were very satisfied and 40 per cent were satisfied. The study also found that 71 per cent of respondents say they would not try to convince other citizens to vote for a political party or candidate.

The situations which are described in relation to Barbados, Jamaica and Trinidad and Tobago are roughly characteristics of most countries in the Caribbean in terms of voter apathy and citizens' faith in the political process and in political leaders themselves. This situation suggests a few things about Caribbean political leaders. First among them is the fact that they are failing in convincing many citizens that they are up to the task. In other words, the data suggest that most citizens are unimpressed by the quality of guidance that leaders are providing. Similarly, they are not convinced of the wisdom of the direction in which their countries are heading, are not being inspired by the messages which leaders are communicating and definitely do not see in the vision being articulated a reason for great hope. This reality represents an invitation to Caribbean leaders to consider what the developmental requirements of leadership are in the current era and what leadership characteristics they are expected to demonstrate. At the heart of this issue are questions of credibility and confidence.

Developing and Demonstrating Leadership

The question raised in the foregoing analysis is: How may leaders of the Caribbean respond to this apparent crisis of confidence their citizens experience? Maxwell (1998), Thompson (2015) and Walter (2015) identify several factors which undermine the faith of followers in leaders in the guidance they seek to give, the direction they take and their capacity to transmit an inspiring vision. These factors include engaging in behaviours which are at odds with their words and engaging in blaming to point out which leader or political party is worse, thereby not asserting that one has done the right thing, but that the other has done a greater wrong. Other behaviours which are cited by authorities as contributing to followers' – citizens and employees – loss of confidence in their leaders is when leaders unapologetically flaunt the law or make unrealistic promises or, though realistic, they do not intend to keep. The core consequence of this kind of conduct is untrustworthiness. The scientific literature, as well as common sense, have repeatedly shown that a leader who cannot be trusted is one, like any person in any other capacity, who is likely to be ineffective and will struggle to gain the regard and confidence of others.

Other theorists also have opinions of what should characterize a leader. Kenneth Blanchard (2010), in his book *Leading at a Higher Level*, argues that accountability is the touchstone of leadership that stands out and is above the ordinary. Blanchard explains that among the behaviours that count as leading at a higher level are the expression of values in behaviours (not words) and delivering on promised performance. Eric Goldman (1952) recounts Teddy Roosevelt saying of his presidency that his office is the "office of moral leadership". This is the high bar to which Caribbean leaders are expected to challenge themselves to rise. According to Bass and Steidlmeier (1999), moral leadership involves being decisive, taking responsibility for actions and leading by example. Thompson (2009) makes a similar case in arguing that the leader ought to be a model of what he or she expects of followers.

Moral leadership, as Bass and Steidlmeier (1999) suggest, is rooted in virtue. Drawing on the Socratic and Confucian tradition, they suggest that the key elements of moral leadership include liberty, utility and distributive justice, which operate alongside the values of transcendence, agency and trust. The elements of moral leadership and the values they create manifest themselves in behaviours such as a leader keeping his or her word, being responsive, demonstrating authenticity by augmenting words with actions, having a strong sense of discernment, seeking to advance the interests of others over seeking self-glory (magnanimity/self-transcendence) and governance approaches which advance the interest of the society or the organization.

Therefore, if the current generation of Caribbean leaders are to be successful in raising the level of public interest in the affairs of their countries, they will have to demonstrate new levels of commitment to accountability, selflessness in public service, improving the structures of governance, being responsive to the needs of citizens and ensuring that public resources are used to advance the good of their countries. These issues come to a head in the global problem of public corruption, which has been manifested regionally and which is briefly examined next.

The Problem of Corruption

The gap between the word of national leaders and their actions with respect to how they treat national resources and the implications of such a gap for corruption is one of the single greatest dangers facing the global economy and, by extension, our national economies. Commonwealth Secretary-General Patricia Scotland warned in May 2018 that corruption is a global tsunami and has suggested that combatting it requires a coordinated international response. She articulates that corruption is poisonous, corrosive, vicious and an enemy of sustainable development which robs the global economy of up to US$2 trillion each year. Edwards (2014) asserts that there is a clarion call across the Caribbean for countries to implement measures to fight corruption in both the public and private sectors. Edwards summarizes arguments put forward on the subject by a leading anti-corruption barrister from the United Kingdom, John McKendrick, who served on the Eastern Caribbean supreme court in the British Virgin Islands. He reports that McKendrick asserts that corruption undermines and weakens the rule of law and, relying on the position held by former chief justice of England and Wales, McKendrick further asserts that the rule of law is essential for economic development.

Transparency International in several of its annual reports supports the view that corruption undermines a country's economy and estimates that corruption sucks at least 5 per cent of Jamaica's GDP, or about US$750 million or J$93 billion, based on Jamaica's 2017 GDP of US$14.77 billion. In the 2017 ranking on the Corruption Perception Index published by Transparency International (2017), Jamaica ranked sixty-eighth. This ranking in 2017 represents a restoration to the place Jamaica held in 2015 after it had fallen fourteen places from sixty-nine to eighty-three in 2016.

Given the cost and pervasiveness of corruption, which, like crime, robs the national economy of resources needed to provide basic social services and support development, there is an urgent need for leaders to take a strong and unequivocal stance against corruption. This problem of corruption, however, is not isolated to Jamaica as a Caribbean country, though among other Caribbean countries Jamaica is one of the worst. That Jamaica ranked sixty-eighth in the 2018 Transparency International report does not compare to the more favourable rankings for five Caribbean countries which are in the top fifty. These are Barbados at twenty-five, Bahamas at twenty-eight, St Vincent and the Grenadines at forty, Dominica at forty-two and St Lucia at forty-eight. The other Caribbean countries ranked were Trinidad and Tobago at 77 and Haiti at 157. These rankings suggest that Barbados and Bahamas are exemplary. Barbados has consistently scored high on the Corruption Perception Index rankings, and while its economy has experienced some setback after the 2008 world recession, those setbacks were generally accepted to be attributable to factors other than corruption (Sandiford 2018).

Given the cost of corruption as has been documented, therefore, it will remain an obstacle to the development of the Caribbean unless drastic steps are taken to root it out, which will include substantial consequences to public officials who are involved in corruption. The conclusion of the foregoing is that corruption represents an exceedingly great cost on a country's economy and as a consequence undermines development. A country's leaders have to provide leadership to any effort to fight corruption. This fight can only be successful if words bemoaning corruption are matched by deeds which promote anti-corruption.

7.

Public Trust

A critical underpinning of any democratic society is public trust. Burrowes (2014), a Guyanese journalist, argues that trust is the glue which holds all interdependent relationships together and that this glue is most critical in the public service. He suggests that outside of the family, the public service is the place in which trust is most important in society. Burrowes further states that there are two dimensions to public trust. The first he says is communal trust. Communal trust has to do with the confidence citizens have in their government that the government will act in their best interest. The mechanism of the public sector is the tool which government is expected to use to fulfil this objective. The second dimension of public trust highlighted by Burrowes relates to the interworking of the different arms of the public service to fulfil their mandate of providing services to the people.

The trust that citizens have in their governments in many countries, including the Caribbean, has been falling. The apathy towards participation in the public service, discussed in the previous chapter, is evidence of the decline in public trust. But the most potent manifestation of the loss of public trust is the perceptions citizens have concerning corruption in government.

The 2019 Global Corruption Barometer report on Latin America and the Caribbean contains seven recommendations, all of which highlight the nexus between public corruption and public trust. These recommendations include

- advocating for stronger political integrity, especially around elections;
- reducing enablers of bribery, especially in the public service;
- strengthening judicial institutions; and
- empowering individuals, civil society, and the media to report corruption.

These recommendations are made against the background of findings such as:

1. The perception that corruption is on the rise across the region, with 53 per cent of all citizens having the view that corruption has increased in the previous twelve months (and only 16 per cent believing it is on the decline). Among the Caribbean countries reported in the survey, Trinidad and Tobago top the adverse ranking, with 62 per cent of

its citizens perceiving that corruption had worsened in the previous twelve months. In second position is Jamaica at 49 per cent, followed by Bahamas at 45 per cent and finally Barbados at 37 per cent.

2. The thinking that governments are not doing enough to deal with corruption, with 57 per cent saying their governments are performing badly in dealing with corruption (39 per cent hold the alternative view).

Perhaps the most definitive finding of the Global Perception Barometer which highlights the depth of the lack of public trust is that more than half of the citizens surveyed believe that presidents, prime ministers and parliamentarians are the most corrupt. In this regard, the Global Perception Barometer survey found that 85 per cent of citizens in Trinidad and Tobago believe their government is corrupt, followed by 80 per cent of Bahamians, 78 per cent of Jamaicans and 53 per cent of Barbadians.

These findings highlight the need for radical steps to be taken by Caribbean governments to deal with corruption and the consequential loss of public trust, if the confidence of citizens in their governments is to be restored and the debilitating impact on development resulting from actual corruption removed.

Another behaviour of public officials which serves to undermine public trust is the lack of selflessness on the part of those who offer themselves for service. Burrowes (2014) highlights this problem in what he describes as the quest for personal advancement being paramount to the provision of service. This occurs when public officials use their office for self-glorification and personal enrichment. This can be seen in anecdotal evidence of politicians and other public servants entering public office with relatively modest assets and despite earning comparatively small salaries compared to counterparts in the private sector, are later assessed to be worth several times what their modest means could have bestowed.

The practice of using public office to advance personal wealth also has to do with greed. There are several reports in various media across the Caribbean of public officials, elected and unelected, who are charged with, and some found guilty of, fleecing the public purse of millions of taxpayer dollars. Blanchard (2010) discusses six other greed-related behaviours apart from pecuniary which undermine trust in leaders. These behaviours include the view that the end always justifies the means, that integrity is negotiable, that power should be used to further one's interest and that it is acceptable to use people to get what one wishes. A leader, whether a politician or otherwise, who operates with this worldview is likely to evoke erosion of trust between himself or herself and others. But as Gannon (2018) and Polka (2018) assert, the display of greed is often imperceptible and functions as a character flaw. This character flaw usually impedes an individual or a leader from achieving excellence, or worse, casts the leader or individual in the light of a tragic hero, propelling him or her to fall from grace. When these outcomes occur, they lead to a loss of trust or damaged relationships. One of the most powerful elements of greed is its compromise of an individual's capacity to truly care for others. Many persons who claim to have a desire to engage in public service are merely using the office to advance personal ambitions, but this lack of care, though not always immediately perceptible, is always present. When the "plot" of self-advancement is uncovered and purported service to others is shown to be self-interest, trust is seriously undermined, both in personal and public relations.

The Jamaican and wider Caribbean public leadership story is not immune from the foregone assertions about greed, self-glory and assuming public positions for personal gratification. Therefore, the suspicion that some of those who seek public office are seeking to advance their interests has been advanced as one of the reasons for voter apathy in Jamaica (Jones 2014) and other Caribbean countries by writers, scholars and public commentators such as Harriott et al. (2013). Harriott et al. found in a number of Latin America Public Opinion Project studies that citizens' trust and participation in political parties are related to (and their perception that the parties represent) their own interests.

In relation to this, Harriott et al., using a points system, found that Belize scored highest, with approximately 62 points on the scale measuring support for the political system, while Suriname scored 61.2, Guyana 58.2, Jamaica 53.6, Trinidad and Tobago 49.7 and Haiti 44.5. These scores reflect the degree to which citizens feel that their individual rights are protected, as well as their pride in the political system. The higher the score, the more favourable the country is viewed by its citizens.

An important measure of how people feel about politicians and the political process can be seen in the participation rates (turnout) in national elections. As has been shown in an earlier chapter, the levels of participation have been falling in a number of Caribbean countries. In Jamaica, there has been a steady decline in turnout over the last twenty years (1997–2016), as shown in table 7.1. Although there was a slight upward movement in 2007 relative to 2002, the general trend has been a steady percentage decline.

While the conduct of public officials in office is to some degree a matter of personal integrity, the correction of the problem of putting personal interest above the public interest and engaging in corrupt behaviour has to be corrected through training, stronger systems of accountability, public pressure

Table 7.1. Voter Turnout in General Elections in Jamaica 1997–2016

Year	Number on Voters' List	Voter Turnout	Percentage
1997	1,182,294	771,068	65.22
2002	1,301,334	768,282	59.04
2007	1,336,307	821,325	61.46
2011	1,648,036	876,310	53.17
2016	1,824,412	882,389	48.37

Source: The Electoral Office of Jamaica

and legislation. To that end, I advance the following corrective measures and interventions:

1. **Mandatory training in political education.** This would include the issues such as local legislation, Jamaica's relations with other countries, international agreements and protocols to which Jamaica is a signatory.
2. **Corruption prevention training and increased sanctions for violations.** This area would involve exposure to issues such as conflicts of interest, arms-length dealings, bases for recusal, accountability in public life and criminal sanctions for certain violations and thus the need to amend or enforce legislation.
3. **Training in ethics and the strengthening of Parliament's ethics committee.** The area of training here may overlap with corruption, but there would be some specific exposure to principles of ethics. In strengthening the ethics committee of Parliament, there should be the establishment of an active oversight mechanism with investigative capabilities. The focus of the work of such a committee should be on preventing the use of public office for the advancement of personal interests and other acts which have the potential to thwart the public good.
4. **Training in public policy, strategic planning and leadership for all members of Parliament and political aspirants**. There should be certain standards of quality representation, one of which is a "representational" plan, also known as a constituency development plan. In order to lead in the process of developing such a plan, the member of Parliament or aspirant should have some experience in the basics of planning, management and leadership. In this regard there would be a need for the establishment of mandatory minimum standards, agreed on a multipartisan or bipartisan basis for persons to be accepted by their political parties to run as representatives.

5. **The establishment of objective representational assessment metrics.** The quality of political representation and the assessment of elected representatives against established metrics on an annual basis should become normative. Non-partisan organizations, comprising diverse professional and even political representatives, would conduct the assessments. The organization should not be dependent on government funding or accept donations from politicians.

6. **Provision for recall of elected representatives.** Representatives who fail to create constituency development plans (which reflect broad-based stakeholder participation) or commit serious ethical violations or are found to be involved in corruption should be recalled through a carefully crafted process.

Impeachment of Public Officials

A final tool of accountability which can be used to restore public trust in governments in the Caribbean is impeachment. Impeachment as a tool of accountability is not practised in Caribbean countries, but as they seek to pursue efforts to strengthen accountability, they should consider using the tool of impeachment, among other sanctions. The practice exists in about twenty-six countries, including Brazil, France, India, Ireland, the Philippines, Russia, South Korea, the United Kingdom and the United States. Interestingly, although laws in the United Kingdom make provision for impeachment, Caribbean countries, which are former colonies of the United Kingdom, do not have such laws.

Therefore, in circumstances in which elected officials fail to conduct themselves properly in office, either through greed, profiting from the office in ways that are unethical or lack of care and attention to the needs of constituents, there should be a provision for impeachment. Following are at least five categories of offences (there could be more) for which parliamentarians should be subject to impeachment proceedings. These are:

1. **Having been found guilty of a high crime or misdemeanour.** This category, as framed in the US Constitution, is about the principle of to whom much is given, much is expected. Thus, something like refusal to pay property taxes, while inexcusable for everyone and punishable by fines and interest, should attract a higher penalty for a legislator.

2. **Involvement in crime or established association with known criminals.** Given the country's high crime rate (though the principle would apply if the level of crime were less), public officials who employ,

associate with, do business with, protect or otherwise act in ways that aid and abet the agenda of criminals should be required to answer for such actions by way of impeachment proceedings.

3. **Lying materially to Parliament or in the submission of information to any organ of the state.** Impeachment should be possible in circumstances in which an elected official states information that is materially important but which turns out to be false. For example, if a public official submits false information on their filings with the Integrity Commission or makes a statement in Parliament which has the effect of misleading the Parliament or the country in critical ways, that elected official should be subject, other things considered, to impeachment proceedings.

4. **Misleading the country in critical matters.** Making false promises to the electorate should be grounds for impeachment. This could arise when a political party commits to taking policy steps that it claims will not have adverse macroeconomic consequences despite there being credible assessments otherwise that show that those policy actions would have adverse economic consequences. Impeachment should also be possible when a government deliberately uses false information as a pretext for undertaking police/military operations, which affect people's rights and freedoms, in a community that is "aligned" with one's political opponents.

5. **Misuse/waste of public funds or use of public funds for personal gain.** When the actions of a public official result in the waste of taxpayers' money and the public official could, or ought to, have exercised control to prevent such waste, or where there is evidence that the funds were used for personal gain, there should be, in addition to possible criminal proceedings, impeachment proceedings.

Suggested Mechanism for Impeachment Proceedings

Given the partisan nature of the parliamentary system of most Caribbean countries (in which decisions and votes are made along party lines), any effective mechanism for impeachment would have to be outside the control of parliamentarians or their hacks. I suggest the following features:

1. Any member of the public or other elected official should be able to initiate impeachment proceedings against or in relation to any elected official. This would require that the initiator makes a submission outlining the facts and circumstances to a designated authority, which would ideally be named the Corruption Prevention and Integrity Commission

(CPIC), as against simply the "Integrity Commission" as is the case in Jamaica, given that an important function of the Integrity Commission is corruption prevention, wherein the Integrity Commission has responsibility for the operationalization of the Corruption Prevention Act. The CPIC, would, as is the case with the Integrity Commission, be headed by a person at the level of a High Court judge and would be staffed with lawyers, senior police officers, forensic auditors, private investigators and other investigative personnel.

2. The CPIC would be active in seeking to have persons who have reports on probable corrupt actions by State actors meet with trusted private investigators to make reports and would conduct investigations to establish the veracity of reports. The CPIC would not pronounce on the weight and implications of the facts – it would simply establish veracity.

3. Upon completion of its investigation the CPIC would make a report to Parliament in which it lays out its factual findings (which could include further facts beyond those submitted by the initiator).

4. Parliament, upon receipt of the report, would then be required to refer the matter to a specially constituted panel of three or five persons, whose selection would be prescribed in law. This panel would include two High Court judges, one of whom would be the chief justice or president of the Court of Appeal. The panel would be empowered to call witnesses, but persons who wish to offer testimony could do so in writing and be cross-examined by lawyers representing the subject of the impeachment proceedings. The panel would produce a report that speaks to the veracity and weight of the allegations and make an unambiguous conclusion concerning the allegations. This report would be tabled in Parliament with one of four recommendations:

   a. Material does not rise to the level warranting impeachment – case dismissed

   b. Material significant to warrant censorship by Parliament

   c. Material of such a nature to warrant removal from office with the prospect of returning to public office in the future

   d. Material of such a nature to warrant removal from office and permanent barring from holding other public office

The relevant laws should also provide that a prime minister be barred from circumventing impeachment proceedings by calling snap elections. Thus, once the process has reached the second stage, it should be made unlawful for the government to call a by-election or a general election. In this regard, a subject's resignation could not obviate or derail an impeachment probe.

Every government has a duty to seek to create and maintain public trust. Those of us with this matter at heart wrestle with how, as a country, we can do a more effective job of creating the conditions for elected officials to act in ways that engender public trust. Keith Burrowes, writing in the *Guyana Chronicle* in February 2014, reminds us that "trust is the glue that holds all interdependent relationships together, and there is probably no more important institution – outside of the family – in which trust is more critical than in the public service" (paragraph 1). The foundational element of public trust revolves around the expectation that a government will act in the best interest of the country. The opposite, of course, is acting in ways that are motivated by personal vested interests or one's political party. When a government acts in ways that are not in the best interest of the country, that important glue disappears and public apathy emerges and mistrust reigns.

8.

Public-Sector Transformation

The problem of a deficit in courage among public servants and other employees and the consequences this deficit portends for society not only require that an appeal be made to leaders at all levels to become courageous but also require that systemic and structural responses be made to support and enable necessary acts of courage. Among the many ways in which the systems and structures can be devised to nurture courage is through implementing certain reforms in the public sector. But public-sector transformation is designed to do more than nurture courage among those who serve – it is expected to result in the delivery of superior service to citizens. In this regard, this chapter examines the role of that key public service functionary known as the "permanent secretary" and discusses a range of actions which governments are being asked to consider, including taking steps to improve, in an overall effort at institutional strengthening of the public service.

The Role of the Permanent Secretary

The permanent secretary is the chief of resource management and accountability in a government ministry. Human resources often consume the single largest share of a ministry's expenditure, in some instances accounting for more than 80 per cent of a ministry's budget. The central place of people management in the operations of a ministry means that transformation of the public sector is a largely people-based process. But more fundamentally, the office which is responsible for the performance of people must be the lynchpin that connects people to expected performance outcomes. In other words, the office of the permanent secretary is the fulcrum of effective public-sector transformation.

Davis (2014a, 2014b) catalogues the establishment of the position of permanent secretary in the governmental arrangements in the Commonwealth, noting that the post had its origins in the United Kingdom in 1830, when Lord Grey took office as prime minister and asked Sir John Barrow, who was secretary of the department of admiralty, to continue serving. This action by Lord Grey ushered in the principle of senior civil servants staying in office on a change of government and serving in a non-partisan way. Davis, in lamenting the practice which emerged in many Commonwealth countries with respect to how the position of permanent secretary is located, is of the view that the governmental arrangements of countries would be more effective if the precedent set by Lord Grey were continued. Instead, Lord Grey's precedent has been eroded over time through legislation and behaviours society has tolerated. Davis contends that in many jurisdictions, the "permanent" had effectively been removed from "permanent secretary", and whereas a permanent secretary was a career civil servant with permanent tenure and not subject to the whims of a minister, he or she may now be removed at will if a minister wishes and gets his or her way.

One effect of the change of the status quo with respect to the stability of tenure of the holder of the office of permanent secretary is that he or she is likely to be less bold and assertive in setting and maintaining standards of accountability. The caution would be predicated on, if in doing so, he or she may offend a staff member whose strong ties to the political party in power makes him or her an untouchable. Davis (2014a, 2014b) discusses the problem, highlighting that many times, the people appointed as heads of agencies and chairs of boards are political heavyweights in the form of party donors, party hacks or persons recommended by them. In some cases, some of these persons are more powerful within the party's apparatus than even the minister. The consequence of this is that neither the minister nor the permanent secretary can hold these people and their associates to account. Should these political heavyweights decide to be corrupt, they can make leadership in the ministry unbearable for the permanent secretary.

One of Jamaica's leading permanent secretaries describes the challenge of seeking to hold political appointees of boards accountable. In an appearance before Parliament's Public Administration and Appropriations Committee on 12 September 2018, Audrey Sewell, permanent secretary in the office of the prime minister, stated, as reported in the *Jamaica Observer* of 13 September 2018, that "permanent secretaries get a lot of flak for things that, by law, we have no authority, no power to address, and it is something that has been recognized and it needs to be addressed because here we are being hauled here to come and account for what happened in one of my agencies". Sewell's assessment may be located on a continuum of possible positions or perspectives a permanent secretary may take in seeking to deal with issues of accountability confronting him or her. Sewell's position may be described as affirmed containment based on law. Davis (2014a, 2014b) accepts that there are indeed structural and political limitations on how far a permanent secretary may go in seeking to exercise oversight. In the same vein, he suggests that there needs to be greater creativity on the part of permanent secretaries in executing their roles. Davis further argues that the containment which permanent secretaries experience is self-imposed. This he attributes to their perception of their own inability to effect change and reinforces the need for them to find creative ways to address the issues which confront them. Davis further suggests that a contributor to less-than-optimum effectiveness on the part of a permanent secretary redounds to their tacit acceptance of the attitude of some ministers. This attitude, she explains, lies in those who believe permanent secretaries have no policy roles except to implement what the minister or the Cabinet decides. He points as well to the attitude of permanent secretaries themselves, who believe they have no creative role in the policy process beyond implementation, and also to a worst-case scenario, which she describes as intellectual laziness in coming up with ideas to improve policy formulation, monitoring and evaluation.

It must be affirmed that as the chief accountable officer, the permanent secretary has a fiduciary obligation to ensure that all funds made available to the ministry are spent in a manner that brings value to the taxpayer. While one accepts that very often a permanent secretary's hands may be tied when it comes to the maintenance of standards with respect of individual instances of resource deployment and accountability, there can be no plausible excuse for not having a system in place to track value for money. This failure does grave injustice to the taxpayer.

In seeking to ensure that the taxpayer gets value for their money, a permanent secretary, in the courageous exercise of his or her technical expertise and fiduciary duties, must ensure that policy decisions of a minister are aligned not to mere, if at all, short-term political advantage but to long-term positive national impact. In this regard a permanent secretary cannot be a political lackey or lapdog. The said exercise of courage and competence should enable a permanent secretary to fearlessly and fairly hold employees in the ministry to the highest standards of accountability without regard for whatever their political leanings may be. At the same time a permanent secretary must be a professional who is above reproach. It must be recognized that permanent secretaries are political creatures as well and thus can fall prey to political agendas that are unrelated to pressure or interference in operational matters by a minister.

To Davis's list of possible reasons permanent secretaries are sometimes not as effective as they might, I would add two other reasons, the one being a lack of courage and the other technical inadequacies. The examples cited in the previous chapter of senior public officials failing to stand up to their political bosses highlight the problem of a lack of courage. Thus, if there are to be radical reforms in the various public sectors of countries of the Caribbean, those who are appointed to head ministries must, in addition to having the security of office, be people who are courageous leaders. But a vital and indispensable accompaniment to courage (which is sometimes, but not always, evinced when security of tenure exists) is competence.

Given the growing practice across many Commonwealth countries in which permanent secretaries, like other senior technical people, are removed from office when a government changes, there is the risk that some of their replacements will be people who are less competent. This risk is particularly high in small developing states, such as Caribbean countries, which do not have a deep talent pool of technically competent people and where highly competent professionals are not particularly eager to assume positions in the public sector. But the path to real transformation of the public sector can be reasonably carved out and maintained with the four key ingredients discussed earlier for which policy measures need to be utilized to secure their achievement. These four ingredients are summarized as follows:

1. The re-affirmation that the permanent secretary is head of the ministry and manager of its resources and must be held accountable for the same.
2. That the permanent secretary must have security of tenure and should not be subject to removal from office based on the whim of an administration which comes to office or a minister who cannot have his or her way.
3. That permanent secretaries develop the capacity for courageous, creative and thoughtful leadership and be willing to challenge the minister when needed, as well as hold all staff accountable, in a fair, just and even-handed manner.
4. That persons selected to be permanent secretaries possess the requisite technical skills to do the job.

Steps towards Public-Sector Transformation

The transformation of the public sector is a critical development imperative, as the public sector is the tool which governments in a well-functioning democracy use to serve the needs of citizens whom they are elected to serve. The following list of transformative actions represents just some of the steps which Caribbean governments are being invited to take. One of the philosophical starting points for the call for public-sector transformation is the need to restore public trust, as discussed in the previous chapter, and thus these steps proposed here are to be seen as part of the overall strategy of improving public trust. The recommendations discussed fall in two broad categories: accountability and efficiency. The argument being advanced therefore is that public-sector transformation must result in stronger systems of accountability and improved efficiency in order for the public sector to be effective, and this in turn will advance public trust.

The proposed steps that are being advanced for meaningful public-sector transformation are as follows:

1. Creating and infusing a culture of excellence
2. Instituting systems of accountability and value for money
3. Strengthening the performance management system
4. Promoting respect for the rule of law and nurturing a culture of reasonableness
5. Digitizing public records
6. Establishing mechanisms for the ongoing performance evaluation of ministries
7. Promoting innovation as a way of life

Creating and Infusing a Culture of Excellence

The creation of a culture of excellence should be the aim of every public and private institution. And where the private ones may falter, government-owned institutions should be held to strict account in this regard. Where this does not exist, deliberate and persistent intervention measures should be initiated to cultivate the required skills and competences, such as knowledge of change management, to develop this culture. Public-sector transformation, then, must be about excellence in service and results. Mergers are mere mechanisms for improved efficiencies and training and development of staff strategies to support excellence. But unless there is an overall reorientation of staff members who believe in excellent performance, not merely getting an excellent appraisal when there is no evidence of actual delivery, there will be no transformation. Excellent service means that the people who are served feel good about the quality of service they receive.

In the 1990s when I worked at the then Telecommunications of Jamaica (TOJ), while other companies were talking about total quality management, TOJ was (brilliantly) exploring and training employees at all levels in total quality culture. What TOJ recognized was that there could be no revolution on management practices outside of a transformed and supportive environment called a culture. People's habits towards and beliefs about internal and external customers had to change if the decision-making processes and modes of the provision of service were to improve. How well TOJ, later Cable and Wireless, did in this regard is for a separate discussion, but the larger point to be understood is that the ethos of an organization has to be supportive of the direction the organization wishes to take.

Another company that focuses on a culture of excellence is the Jamaica Money Market Brokers Group. It even has a post of "Group Executive Director of Culture and Human Development", which signals how seriously they take this critical need. Donna Duncan-Scott, who holds that post, focuses a significant amount of her energy on maintaining and deepening the culture of love, respect and accountability that the company's late founder, Joan Duncan, emphasized and epitomized. One of the principles of total quality culture was that "leadership must lead", that is, they should model in their behaviours, including their approaches to decision-making and attitudes to internal customers, the kinds of standards they demand of employees. At TOJ, the training in total quality culture began at the top with the senior executives. Very often when I do the training in companies and ministries, one of the recommendations that participants make on the evaluation form is that their managers or heads of department or other senior people should be exposed to the training. The attainment of real reform in the public sector requires as a first step that permanent secretaries lead the way by consistently showing through precept and practice that excellence is the only acceptable standard.

Value for Money and Accountability

Okech (2017) suggests that the issue of value for money in public service has become a contentious and very prominent subject in the development agenda within both developed and developing economies. It is thus arguable that given the increasing concern about how public officials handle public funds, one critical frontier for public discourse is the twin of value for (taxpayers') money and accountability.

One area in which Caribbean governments spend a substantial amount of money is in the training of public-sector workers. The Ministry of Finance in Jamaica reports that between 2010 and 2017 the Jamaican government spent over J$1.4 billion on the training of 1,453 civil servants. At J$1.4 billion and with approximately 1,400 civil servants trained, the expenditure per trainee is in the region of J$1 million. Using the 2016 Civil Service Establishment as a reference point, which shows that there are some 34,290 operational posts in the civil service, and using this figure as the average for the period 2010–17, it means that the 1,453 civil servants represented a mere 4 per cent of the total establishment. The upshot is that across two political administrations an alarming J$1 million per person was spent on training less than 5 per cent of the civil servant population, excluding what is spent on teachers.

With this massive amount of spending by government and in keeping with accountability, government should endeavour to make clear in what areas the training services were delivered and those in receipt are deployed for maximum benefit for the country. Additionally, the government should ensure strict tested and proven accountability standards are in place to measure the impact on the investment. But this is an area in which improvement needs to be made. Coming back to the case of Jamaica, Johnson (2017) reports that Wayne Jones head of the Jamaica Civil Service Association and a deputy financial secretary in the Ministry of Finance and the Public Service, has acknowledged that there is no system in place to track the impact of expenditure on training. Checks with other Caribbean countries and in other parts of the world might very well reveal similar gaps, but all hope is not lost. In instances where there is currently no accountability mechanism in place, it is not too late to implement some, provided that the government commitment to ensure value for money is not in rebuke of the same.

The path to substantive and sustainable public-sector transformation must involve the establishment of a culture in which the principle of a "return on investment" (which has both qualitative and quantitative measures) must become the primary consideration in the use of public funds. Alongside that principle will have to be a commitment to sanctions for persons who have charge of taxpayer funds and who deploy these but are unable to show the value received. They in return must be held accountable, including the requirement to repay those funds or be barred from handling public funds in the future.

Strengthening Performance Management

Given the current state of the public sector, which is a place where people can find refuge when they either want easy money or cannot find a job elsewhere, its image must be changed by developing a new culture. It must become a place where one is admitted because of a track record of performance or a presumption of the capacity to perform. The public sector must be known for having clearly defined performance targets for those employed, with reasonably rigorous standards, and for terminating the services of those who do not perform. In this regard leadership must lead by example.

Thus, regardless of which party is in power, each minister of government should have a job description to which the public must have access. This strategic tool will give them a better grasp of their portfolios and provide a clear context of functions and deliverables in which their performance can be measured against these performance criteria. Taken seriously, this will no doubt help to improve performance, especially when accompanied by reasonable sanctions for non-performance. A job description for ministers of government alone will not result in public-sector transformation. It requires that, in addition to job descriptions for ministers, there would be results-focused job descriptions for their permanent secretaries and all employees across all levels. This would be accompanied by a strict performance management system in which a score of 88 per cent or 95 per cent (which are common occurrences), as well as the not-too-few cases of 101 per cent, are supported by evidence of the value added.

How could governments achieve these suggestions? Having established permanent ministries and results-focused job descriptions, the government would need to ensure that there is an independent body that assesses the performance of each ministry on an ongoing basis. This body would serve an auditing function like that of the auditor general. But while the auditor general looks at the ministry or agency at the strategic level, there is need for some other mechanism which would do spot and random reviews of performance management reports. The purpose of such reviews would be to test veracity, uncover supportive evidence to substantiate performance scores, and to examine whether promotions or other rewards are warranted. This office could be located in the office of the auditor general.

Promoting Respect for the Rule of Law and Nurturing a Culture of Reasonableness

A society that is governed by the rule of law is one that says that lawful acts are grounded in principles to which all citizens will subscribe. When actions either by "ordinary" citizens or elected officials run afoul of those principles, there should be consequences. Imposing consequences does not mean firing people, hounding them out of office or locking them up for the least of infractions. Respect for the rule of law means that there is a standard by which we measure the probity of conduct, and when there are deviations there should be public conversation so as to ensure we are clear regarding what the expected behaviour should be, as well as appropriate sanctions which may be mild, moderate or severe. Public officials, in descending order of authority, have the foremost responsibility for ensuring that respect is shown for the rule of law. Thus, the governor general and, after him, the prime minister has the highest duty to show regard for the rule of law. In Jamaica, two judgments handed down by the Privy Council in 2017 bring into sharp focus the issue of respect for the rule of law and the need to promote a culture of reasonableness in the public sector as part of efforts to transform the sector. Although one of the cases originated in a private company, the lessons are applicable to the public sector.

Two recent judgments by the UK-based Privy Council, which were first heard by Jamaica's Industrial Disputes Tribunal (IDT), provide important insights into Jamaica's Labour Relations and Industrial Disputes Act and the meaning and importance of reasonableness. Most other Caribbean countries have employment legislation which sets out the rights of workers to fair treatment. Even in the absence of specific legislation, there are litigable rights that every Caribbean citizen has under common law and under the principles of natural justice and for which the doctrine of reasonableness applies.

The two cases are National Commercial Bank (NCB) versus the IDT and the University of Technology versus the IDT. Both rulings were handed down in July 2017 by the UK-based Privy Council and are therefore binding on all countries in the British Commonwealth. In my assessment, there are four key lessons from both rulings, namely:

1. The IDT is not just an appeals tribunal restricted merely to determining whether the processes used by an employer in terminating the services of an employee were fair; the IDT is a body with an original jurisdiction empowered to conduct its own hearing and to determine not only if processes were fair but also whether a decision was justified.

2. An employee's livelihood, like their liberty and life, is part of his or her property. In the same way that the state cannot lawfully take away a person's liberty or life without due process, an employer cannot lawfully take away a person's job capriciously or high-handedly simply because it was issued by the employer in the first place.

3. The established grievance and disciplinary procedures that an organization has in place are not beyond the reach of the IDT, regardless of how well entrenched they are. If the IDT finds that those procedures breach the principles of natural justice, no action taken using those procedures can stand.

4. The Labour Relations and Industrial Disputes Act in fact shields the IDT from having its decisions overturned except on a point of law. This means no court, not even the Privy Council, can interfere with a decision of the IDT based on the IDT's interpretation of facts or determine what facts the IDT should have considered in deciding a matter.

This case started out as Jennings versus NCB. Jennings was employed at NCB for thirty-three years. Sometime in 2014 he was accused by the bank of approving four loans totalling just over J$48 million, which turned out to be bad loans, and as a consequence, the bank terminated his services. The process by which his services were terminated raised questions for the IDT. Jennings was instructed one evening to appear before a panel the following morning to answer charges of dereliction of duty. The panel included his immediate supervisor, his supervisor's supervisor and the bank's lawyer. The charges against him were drafted by his supervisor. Jennings was not represented, as employees at the level of manager in the bank are not unionized.

The IDT in its ruling found, among other things, that

1. The notice given to Jennings was not adequate, as he was given only a couple hours' notice.
2. The said persons who laid the charges against him were the same persons who tried him. (While this method is consistent with the bank's disciplinary procedures, the IDT held that such a procedure breached a sacred principle of due process, namely that a person cannot be a judge in his own cause.)
3. The decision to terminate Jennings's service was unjustified with regard to all the facts of the case.

The bank challenged the decision of the IDT at the level of the Supreme Court and lost. The bank took the matter to the Court of Appeal and later the Privy Council and lost on both occasions. Thus, the ruling of the IDT that NCB pay Jennings 220 weeks of salary is final.

Among the arguments advanced by NCB before the courts was that the IDT erred when it found that the decision to terminate Jennings was unjustified, contending that such a determination was outside the remit of the IDT. Both the Supreme Court and the Court of Appeal disagreed with the bank.

This UTECH case is beautifully summarized in the opening paragraph of the judgment and captures the salient questions, namely, whether the "IDT can take into account matters of which the employer was unaware at the time of the dismissal" of an employee and whether the IDT "can form its own judgment (concerning) whether in light of all the information available, the dismissal was justifiable".

The facts here are complex but essentially concern whether the employee had permission to be absent from work. The evidence shows that the employee had applied for vacation leave a month in advance and submitted her application to her supervisor, who had not signed the form until after she had already gone on leave. This signing was done when the supervisor took the form to the human resources department and asked what he should do with it. In addition, the employee was absent from work for two discrete periods after her vacation leave, but these periods were covered by applications for sick leave, which she made accompanied by medical certificates. The employee was initially suspended pending an investigation. The union took the matter to the Ministry of Labour, and while the matter was pending before the ministry, UTECH amended the charges and held a disciplinary hearing resulting in the termination of the services of the employee.

The key issue here is that the IDT in its ruling held that, given the facts of the case, including issues of which UTECH was not aware at the time it dismissed the employee, the decision to terminate was unjustified. UTECH, on the other hand, contended that given what it knew at the time of its decision to terminate, the decision was justified and as such the IDT ought not to have interfered with the decision.

The binding judgment of the Privy Council is that the IDT has the authority to determine whether an employer's decision to terminate the services of an employee is justified and that the IDT in making a ruling has the authority to consider facts of which an employer may not be aware at the time the employer made its decision.

Both employees and employers owe it to themselves and each other, as well as their organizations and the wider society, to be reasonable. Reasonableness is so central to business and human interactions that a large body of knowledge (specifically administrative law) is built upon it. The doctrine is located in the body of knowledge known as Wednesbury's Law, which defines what constitutes an unreasonable decision. The thinking has evolved to be framed as one in which unreasonableness is a decision that is so outrageous and irrational that no right-thinking person or tribunal would make such a decision. Thus, in everyday relationships and in the practice of the law, reasonableness is vital.

Yet despite the importance of reasonableness in interpersonal and legal dealings, lawyers often find themselves trying to make out on behalf of their clients that self-evidently unreasonable acts are reasonable. What I often find curious about how lawyers do their job is that depending on the side they are arguing, the very act they condemned in once case, they likely defend in the other. Thus, if Jennings had retained the lawyers retained by NCB, although the facts would remain the same, they would argue the opposite of what they fought all the way to the Privy Council. This issue raises the question of intellectual honesty. Intellectual dishonesty may very well be an occupational hazard of the legal profession. That this may be so exposes the larger question of the kind of society we wish to create and, more subversively, the kind of human being and professional that one is. Is there a role for a lawyer to advise a client that his or her case is without merit? Does the expenditure made by the bank in fighting the decision of the IDT tell us anything about the values (the soul) of the bank?

Imagine what it would mean for employees if it were legally permissible for an employer to give an employee less than twenty-four hours' notice to appear before a panel to defend him or herself, unaided and unaccompanied, and tried by the same people who charged him or her with wrongdoing. It would mean that every employee is at risk. Imagine what it would mean if it were deemed reasonable in law for an employer to dismiss an employee at will on some pretext using due process and all that the IDT could do is examine whether proper procedures were followed without reference to whether the decision was justified.

These recent rulings are clarion calls for reasonableness in the workplace. What the judgments mean is that if employers do not put proper procedures in place and act reasonably, there is recourse through the labour laws for employees to seek redress, which is a far less expensive route than the court. The framers of the Labour Relations and Industrial Disputes Act have left a firewall of protection for workers, and these two rulings of the Privy Council have put a steel fence over that firewall.

Both cases are relevant to all Commonwealth countries, and therefore governments of the Caribbean are urged to extract the lessons from these cases as they seek to advance the principles of fairness in the operations of their public sectors. The issue of reasonableness is fundamental to trust. If employees and citizens do not have confidence that public officials will be reasonable in their actions, they will not be willing or able to trust them (Hurley 2006).

Digitizing Public Records

Many people will be able to identify with the "can't find the file" excuse/explanation often given when one is doing business with a public-sector entity. Some people have had to resubmit hard-to-obtain documents time and again. Many business transactions are delayed and a whole host of difficulties encountered. In order to achieve real public reform, one crucial step which must be taken is the digitization of public records and the seamless access to those records, with perhaps a few exceptions, by all public-sector entities.

There are several self-evident advantages to digitizing public records. These include increased productivity, as less time will be spent trying to "find" paper files, easy accessibility, enhanced security, enhanced information preservation, improved space management and enhanced disaster recovery (Aptara Corp. 2018).

Promoting Innovation as a Way of Life

Based on the challenges giving rise to the need for public-sector reform and the possible solutions already advanced, the efforts to get it that way have to be wide and varied. A similar sentiment was echoed by the OECD in a 2017 report entitled "Fostering Innovation in the Public Sector". It points out that the nature and scale of public-sector challenges require governments to develop a response that goes beyond incremental process improvements. An improved public sector must be focused on radical changes, not mere tinkering. In this regard, innovation, which contemplates engaging the creative energies of employees, must become a way of life. It thus follows that in order to achieve this "way of life" status, governments are expected to create an environment which promotes innovative behaviours and that which rewards these acts of innovative spirit.

The report identifies four concrete actions which governments need to take in order to create an innovative public sector. These are investing in civil servants, facilitating the free flow of information, designing new organizational structures which emphasize partnerships and establishing rules and processes that enable innovation. A critical precondition for maximizing the value of the investments in civil servants must be, as was discussed earlier in this chapter, the establishment of mechanisms for recording which civil servants have been trained in what skills and determining their place of assignment in the service at any given time. An equally critical consideration must be the creation of evaluative tools to enable permanent secretaries to assess the value that these civil servants are adding towards advancing the innovation agenda.

The OECD acknowledges that the notion of innovation is contrary to the bureaucratic mindset on which the public sector is built and the political and organizational mandate to deliver services in a consistent way. While consistency needs to be guaranteed in order to safeguard the rights of citizens, the tension between taking risks, on the one hand, and operating in a relatively stable and predictable context, on the other, needs to be held in a creative space.

Another important element of fostering innovation in the public service is the changing of mindsets concerning traditional notions of power and authority. Subsequently, the changes in organizational structures that must be undertaken in any drive towards innovation will have to involve removal of, or adjustments to, the hierarchical reporting arrangements which exist in most civil service establishments. Yet another cultural mindset change that will have to be pursued by governments which are seeking to transform their public sectors is that of focusing more on productivity than on production, as well as time efficiency rather than time volume. These two issues are explored in further depth in chapter 9.

A large part of the reason public-sector transformation has been so elusive for many countries is that established systems, processes and cultures are hard to reshape, and thus starting over is sometimes an easier way of creating new approaches. The OECD highlights this challenge, noting that with the mandate that governments have to continually provide services, the solution to the competing demands to change and innovate while maintaining the status quo means that parallel structures have to co-exist. In this structure, the new is being established alongside the old, and as the old is gradually phased out, the ethos of the new is phased in.

9.

Courageous Leadership
An Appeal

The concern about the quality of representation and, by extension, the quality of governance offered by political leaders and the consequence that these issues have for the development of the Caribbean triggers the question of the role of leadership in achieving the desired ends of quality governance and development. It was argued in chapter 7 that impeachment is one of the remedies which Caribbean countries should pursue in seeking to ensure that elected officials are held accountable. In addition to impeachment, which is a final resort option, is a more ongoing tool, and that is courageous leadership which public servants who serve in non-elected offices should provide.

People who hold power, particularly the power of political office, do not generally submit to the authority and control of others willingly (Galbraith 1983). This means that the degree of influence which public servants will be able to exercise over the actions of their political "bosses" will be derived from both courage and skilful communication, contingent on having earned the respect of these political bosses. This chapter examines the nature of courageous leadership and its importance as a tool of development in the Caribbean.

The need to assert and unearth the value of courageous leadership is based in part on the fact that courageous leadership is not a common quality in the public service. Pena (2017) describes a courageous leader as one who guides staff without stamping out creativity and leads by example. Pena suggests that courageous leadership is expressed in three forms: try courage, trust courage and tell courage. "Try" courage, she suggests, is the determination to undertake a task never before undertaken and where the risk of failure is high. "Trust" courage is the behaviour on the part of the leader in which he or she is willing to relinquish power and delegate to others in circumstances in which those to whom power and responsibility have been delegated may fail to deliver. "Tell" courage is represented by the capacity to speak about one's beliefs and convictions in contexts in which doing so may make others uncomfortable and, by extension, involves risks to one's position in the organization.

The type of courageous leadership demanded of public servants in Caribbean countries is generally of the third type. It is the kind of courage that carries the risk of being fired or side-lined or passed over for a promotion. In practice, "tell" courage is seen in the conduct of the public servant, whether the permanent secretary or other employees who will tell a minister that while what he or she is seeking to do may be noble and necessary, the route being taken is illegal or unethical. Here is a prime example of what this means. Former secretary of state of the United States, Rex Tillerson, in a famous interview carried on NBC in December 2018, relates that on a number of occasions he had to tell President Trump that while he understood what he was trying to achieve, the way he was going about it was in violation of the law. Tillerson is one of many senior Trump administration officials who was pushed out by the president. The disclosures made by Tillerson give a look into why he was not kept on by Trump and why Tillerson could not remain in the Cabinet. "Tell" courage carries a cost for the courageous leader, but his or her decision is usually guided by the public's best interest – a price which is always worth it.

Yet another example comes out of the United States. Secretary of Defense General Mattis also displayed profound "tell" courage in his letter of resignation from the Trump administration. In it he made it clear to the president that their values were at odds and that he (Mattis) was not prepared to sacrifice his core beliefs and principles in the interest of Trump's agenda. The conduct of Tillerson and Mattis is not only a testament to their personal courage but an example to other public servants not only in the United States but across the world. Mandela (2018) offers the counsel that courage is not fearlessness, but the will and determination to stand for what one believes and speak as one is convinced even though feeling a sense of fear.

Jamaica has also seen some "tell" courage leaders. Actually, there are three former public servants in Jamaica who were known for their courage. They are Gordon Wells, Herbert Walker and, most recently, Colin Bullock. The *Gleaner* in its editorial of 20 October 2017 paid tribute to the skill, competence, integrity and courage of these three men. The paper noted that while they were respectful to their political bosses, they did not display the obsequiousness that is all too common today in the face of ministerial overreach and expropriation of authority. These men displayed what Pena (2017) calls "tell" courage, as they spoke truth to power and were clear about, and insisted on, the line of demarcation between the minister as the political executive and the permanent civil service.

In speaking of Walker at his funeral, in 2017 former prime minister P.J. Patterson recounted instances in which Walker reminded him that he (Walker) was responsible for operations, while Patterson was responsible for policy.

Speaking of Gordon Wells, the *Gleaner* in its 17 October 2017 editorial stated that Wells was a man of deep integrity, the likes of whom ought to be examples for today's public servants, who have ceded too much of their authority to encroaching politicians.

Former minister of finance Peter Phillips in 2017 described Bullock in similar terms in commenting on his passing, highlighting that he was both gracious and fearless in dealing with members of the political directorate. The *Gleaner* in its 20 October 2017 editorial described Bullock as an example and likened him to Walker and Wells in terms of his fearlessness, professionalism, competence and commitment to doing the right thing.

It is instructive that despite their record of quality public service they are not celebrated except by a handful of close friends, and the examples they have set are not placed before the country as the way all public servants are expected to behave, as most civil servants avoid crossing the paths of ministers in a display of what I have called cowardism, which I characterize as the antithesis of courage.

Cowardism with Examples from Jamaica

Cowardism is not a word that has as yet been accepted into the lexicon of the English language. I define cowardism as the state of being, or the choice to be, a coward and defending that position as a philosophical way of living. It is the difference between being afraid and not even being aware that one is acting or speaking based on fear, or knowing that one is afraid and admitting the same painfully and without pleasure and adopting a stance of not doing the right thing out of fear and arguing for the legitimacy of that position. In this regard cowardism is the philosophy of cowards.

Cowardism is manifested in the obeisance of public servants who are afraid to challenge their boss by the friendly reporting, or sometimes non-reporting, of people in the media who seek to protect privileged positions; in church members who are unwilling to take a stance against destructive actions of their leaders; and by public servants who are afraid to question policy decisions and other actions of governments even when it is self-evident that the policies are flawed or the actions contrary to rules. Cowardism occurs when a public servant has data or other information that challenges the validity or accuracy of a position taken by an elected official but who conceals that information out of fear that he or she may lose his or her job.

Now let us be clear, cowardism is not the greatest sin, nor is courage the only virtue. But the default thinking of many that "the coward man keeps sound bones" has perhaps done more harm to organizations and societies than any other handicap that people possess. The long-awaited new day in public life that we desire in Jamaica will only come when as citizens, employees, professionals, church members and family members, we acquire the courage to hold ourselves and each other accountable. There are some characteristics about courage we should ponder. The capacity and willingness to display courage do not mean that one is a paragon of perfection. It is also not the case that the display of courage will release or protect one from misfortune; from being misunderstood; or from facing derision, setback and abuse.

In the 1990s during the trial of a former minister of government in relation to funds from the Overseas Farm Work Programme, the then permanent secretary was asked during the trial about the advice given to the minister. The essence of the response was that a permanent secretary could not be expected to direct the minister on how to conduct himself. In 2017 there was another public display of cowardism involving the police commissioner, who had expressed support for recommendations contained in a report on a police operation known as the "Tivoli Invasion". An even more egregious act of cowardism was displayed by the leadership of the National Works Agency. In probing a J$600 million public works project undertaken under the titular direction of the agency during a ten-day period before the local government elections of 2016, the Office of the Contractor General in a 2017 report found that the leadership of the National Works Agency had advised the Cabinet that works of that kind usually cost in the region of J$100 million. But despite the agency's technical and experiential advice, the Cabinet proceeded to allocate J$600 million for the project and did so in violation of the procurement guidelines. In its display of cowardism, the leadership of the National Works Agency offered no objection or contrary advice to the government.

The lack of courageous leadership by the administrations of both political parties has been a dominant feature of governance and politics in Jamaica for decades, with severe consequences for the country. For example, the pace of social change pursued by the Manley administration of the 1970s did not have the full support of some senior public servants, but few were willing to speak boldly to the administration to propose a more measured pace. The consequence was that the change was chaotic. Similarly, the pace at which the government implemented the reform of the financial sector in the 1990s did not have the full blessing of the technocrats, but few were willing to speak bluntly until after the collapse of the sector, which had catastrophic consequences for the economy.

Traits of Courageous Leaders

Apart from the characteristics named by Pena (2017), other theoreticians have fielded different traits that cohere to form the composite of a courageous leader. For example, Tardanico (2013) discusses ten traits of courageous leadership, all of which are applicable to the reality of cowardism in public life in various countries, not only Jamaica. Among the traits explored by Tardanico are:

1. **The willingness to seek feedback and listen**. It remains the case that one of the most important soft attributes of a courageous leader is the willingness to expose his or her views to scrutiny and analysis and to engage feedback on same. In doing so, the leader is saying by behaviour that he or she is open to criticism and correction and is willing to change his or her mind in the face of compelling wisdom articulated by others.

2. **The capacity to say what needs to be said**. On the other hand, a leader shows he or she is fearless and willing to sacrifice himself or herself when he or she is capable of expressing what needs to be said. In this regard, it is helpful to recognize that leadership is not a position. Rather, it is a behaviour as well as the capacity to influence. Thus, the person exercising the courage to speak what needs to be spoken is often not the chair of a committee or the head of an organization, but another from down below who is undaunted by the prospect of being side-lined for having spoken.

3. **Taking action on performance issues**. A large part of the problem with public service in Jamaica is that few face consequences for underperformance. Whenever it does happen that an underperformer faces consequences, it is more often than not for reasons unrelated to performance, but the issue of underperformance serves as a convenient facade.

4. **Giving credit to others**. Courageous leaders know that they are not omnipotent or omniscient, and thus they are not fazed by the idea that others (including their opponents or predecessors in office) may be better at some things than they are or may know more about some things than they do. But more importantly, they know that they can benefit from the ideas of others. It is a cowardly and insecure leader who is unable to praise members of his or her team for the contribution of his or her opponents.

5. **Holding others and oneself accountable**. A leader must, if he or she is to have a meaningful impact, hold others accountable. But the moral authority to hold others accountable rests not in the power of office but in the profile of personal accountability. Any leader, whether a prime minister, chief executive officer or other who is not personally accountable does not have the moral authority to hold even the bearer accountable.

Courage cannot be legislated or otherwise mandated, but it is a necessary quality for the handling of the complex and complicated issues facing society. Given the systemic social and structural problems faced by Caribbean societies, it will take courageous leadership to tackle those problems. Among those systemic, social and structural problems is corruption, which, as has been shown, is a major obstacle to the development of the Caribbean. The same is true about crime, as well as about the resoluteness to address the deficiencies in the education system and investing the necessary resources to transform the same. This book therefore not only calls for radical policy steps to address the pressing social, cultural and political problems facing the Caribbean but also calls for the moral quality of courage to do the difficult and unpopular things which need to be done in order to advance the development of the region.

References

Allaire, Jason. 2018. "Five Issues Facing Higher Education in 2018". *Cornerstone Blog*. 15 January. https://www.cornerstone.edu/blogs/lifelong-learning-matters/post/five-issues-facing-higher-education-in-2018.

Al-Rodhan, Nayef, and Gérard Stoudmann. 2006. "Definitions of Globalization: A Comprehensive Overview and a Proposed Definition". Report. Program on the Geopolitical Implications of Globalization and Transnational Security. 6 June.

Altbach, Philip G., and Jane Knight. 2007. "The Internationalization of Higher Education: Motivations and Realities". *Journal of Studies in International Education* 11, no. 3–4: 290–305.

Aptara Corp. 2018. "Latest Thinking: 10 Advantages of Digitization and Data Capture You Must Know". https://www.aptaracorp.com/blog/10-advantages-digitization-and-data-capture-you-must-know.

Bank of Jamaica. 2011. "Historic Rates of the Jamaican Dollar to the US Dollar". http://www.boj.org.jm/uploads/news/speech_-_jcc_luncheon,_2011-9-13.pdf.

Barbados Election Centre. 2018. "Election Results 1951–Present". *Caribbean Elections*. 12 December. http://www.caribbeanelections.com/bb/elections/default.asp.

Bass, Bernard M., and Paul Steidlmeier. 1999. "Ethics, Character, and Authentic Transformational Leadership Behavior". *Leadership Quarterly* 10, no. 2: 181–217.

Beckford, George. 1972. *Persistent Poverty: Underdevelopment in Plantation Economies of the Third World*. New York: Oxford University Press.

Bernal, Richard. 2019. "The Globalization of Higher Education: The Imperative for a Caribbean Regional Cluster". *Caribbean Journal of Education* 41, no. 1: 1–52.

Blanchard, Ken. 2010. *Leading at a Higher Level: Blanchard on Leadership and Creating High Performing Organizations*. London: FT Press.

Boham, Hector, and Sam Rockson Asamoah. 2011. "Corruption and Fraud Audit Consortium (CAFAC) Ghana Limited". *Ghana Web*. 17 April. https://www.ghanaweb.com/GhanaHomePage/NewsArchive/Corruption-and-Fraud-Audit-Consortium-CAFAC-Ghana-Limited-207110#.

Bunting, Peter. 2013. "Statement by the Minister of National Security". http://bunting.org.jm/wp-content/uploads/speeches/JIS_Statement_on_Crime_by_Minister_Bunting_Sept_2013.pdf.

Burns, James MacGregor. 1978. *Leadership*. New York: Harper and Row.

Burrowes, Keith. 2014. "Importance of Public Trust". *Guyana Chronicle*. 15 February. http://guyanachronicle.com/2014/02/15/importance-of-public-trust.

Callaghan, Brett. n.d. "1st Prime Minister Errol Barrow 1966–1976". *Totally Barbados*. https://www.totallybarbados.com/articles/about-barbados/people/barbados-prime -ministers/1st-prime-minister-errol-barrow/. Accessed 3 April 2020.

Calmera, Runy, and Miguel Goede. 2015. "12 Challenges Facing Caribbean Small Island Developing States". *Caribbean Journal*. 8 March. https://www.caribjournal.com/2015 /03/08/12-challenges-facing-caribbean-small-island-developing-states/.

Cammaerts, Bart. 2015. "Social Media and Activism". *LSE Research Online*. https:// onlinelibrary.wiley.com/doi/abs/10.1002/9781118767771.wbiedcs083.

Caribbean Policy Research Institute. 2009. "Funding Tertiary Education in Jamaica: Background Brief". *Caribbean Policy Research Institute*. 16 November. https://docs .google.com/viewerng/viewer?url=http://www.capricaribbean.org/sites/default/files /public/documents/briefing_paper/funding_tertiary_education_in_jamaica.pdf.

Chanda, Rupa. 2002. "Movement of Natural Persons and the GATS: Major Trade Policy Impediments". In *Development, Trade and the WTO: A Handbook*, edited by Bernard Hoekman, Aaditya Mattoo and Philip English, 302–14. Washington, DC: World Bank.

Chi, Wei, Richard Freeman and Hongbin Li. 2015. "Education Attainment and the Labour Market in China, 1989–2013". Paper presented at the fourth SOLE/EALE World Meetings. Montreal, Canada. 26–28 June. https://www.sole-jole.org/15289 .pdf. Accessed 3 April 2020.

Clarke, Colin. 2006. Politics, Violence and Drugs in Kingston, Jamaica. *Bulletin of Latin American Research* 25:420–40. 10.1111/j.0261-3050.2006.00205.x.

Coleman, David. 2003. "Quality Assurance in Transnational Education". *Journal of Studies in International Education* 7, no. 4: 354–78.

Collier, Paul, and David Dollar. 2002. *Globalization, Growth, and Poverty: Building an Inclusive World Economy*. Washington, DC: World Bank and Oxford University Press.

Collins, J. 2006. "Big Issues Facing CARICOM". *Caribbean 360*. 3 July. http://www .caribbean360.com/news/big-issues-facing-caricom.

Coombs, Michael. 2018. "Fatherlessness Raises Crime Risk". *Gleaner*. 24 June. http:// jamaica-gleaner.com/article/commentary/20180624/michael-coombs-fatherlessness -raises-crime-risk.

Córdova, José Ernesto López, and Juan Rebolledo Márquez Padilla. 2016. "Productivity in Mexico: Trends, Drivers, and Institutional Framework". *International Productivity Monitor* 30:28.

Cross-Border Education Research Team. 2017. "Branch Campuses". 20 January. http:// cbert.org/branch-campus/.

Csiszar, John. 2019. "Ten Fastest-Growing Industries to Invest in This Year". 30 July. https://www.gobankingrates.com/investing/stocks/fastest-growing-industries-to -invest-in/.

Davis, Carlton. 2014a. "Permanent Secretaries and Accountability (Pt 1)". *Gleaner*. December 14. http://jamaica-gleaner.com/article/focus/20141214/permanent -secretaries-and-accountability-pt-1-0.

———. 2014b. "Permanent Secretaries and Accountability (Pt 2)". *Gleaner*. 21 December. http://jamaica-gleaner.com/article/news/20141221/permanent-secretaries-and -accountability-part-2.

della Porta, Donnatella, and Mario Diani. 2006. *Social Movements: An Introduction*. 2nd ed. Oxford: Blackwell.

de Moll, K.E. 2010. "Everyday Experiences of Power". PhD dissertation, University of Tennessee.

Dicken, Peter. 1992. *Global Shift: The Internationalization of Economic Activity*. London: Chapman.

Drori, Gili S., Markus A. Höllerer and Peter Walgenbach. 2014. "Unpacking the Glocal-ization of Organization: From Term, to Theory, to Analysis". *European Journal of Cultural and Political Sociology* 1, no. 1: 85–99.

Dujon, Daryl. 2013. "10 Steps to Chronic Underdevelopment". *Caribbean Centre for Research on Trade and Development Blog*. 16 August. http://www.ccrtd.org/blog /2013/8/19/10-steps-to-chronic-underdevelopment#.XJsf2fZFzIU=.

EC-OECD. 2012. "A Guiding Framework for Entrepreneurial Universities". 18 December. https://www.oecd.org/site/cfecpr/EC-OECD%20Entrepreneurial%20Universities %20Framework.pdf.

Edwards, Al. 2014. "Fighting Corruption in the Caribbean". *Jamaica Observer*. 21 February. http://www.jamaicaobserver.com/business/Fighting-corruption-in -the-Caribbean_16117668.

Ellington, Owen. 2019. "Exploring the Impacts of the Gang Subculture". Panel discussion on gang culture, Kingston, Jamaica.

Faust, Drew Gilpin. 2010. "The Role of the University in a Changing World". Speech. Royal Irish Academy, Trinity College, Dublin. 30 June.

Florea, Ramona, and Radu Florea. 2013. "Entrepreneurship and Education in European Union Countries". *Economy Trandisciplinarity Cognition* 16, no. 2: 75–80. https:// www.researchgate.net/publication/315768505_Entrepreneurship_and_Education _in_European_Union_Countries/citation/download.

Frater, Terence. 2015. "Jamaica's Policy Toward GATS". *International Higher Educa-tion* 53:13–14. https://ejournals.bc.edu/ojs/index.php/ihe/article/viewFile/8052 /7203.

Galbraith, J.K. 1983. *The Anatomy of Power*. Boston: Houghton Mifflin Harcourt.

Galston, William. 2018. "The Rise of European Populism and the Collapse of the Center-Left". https://www.brookings.edu/blog/order-from-chaos/2018/03/08/the -rise-of-european-populism-and-the-collapse-of-the-center-left/.

Gannon, Mary Lee. 2018. "The 7 Deadly Sins Leaders Commit that Hold Them Back". *Ladders*. 16 May. https://www.theladders.com/career-advice/the-7-deadly-sins -leaders-commit-that-hold-them-back.

Geffert, Kerry. 2018. "International Student Enrollments: Embracing the Challenge". http://www.terradotta.com/newsletter-article-7-2018.

"General Elections Are Set to Be Held in Trinidad and Tobago in Autumn 2015". *Oxford Business Group*. 2015. https://oxfordbusinessgroup.com/overview/general -elections-are-set-be-held-trinidad-and-tobago-autumn-2015.

Giovanini, Adilson, and Marcelo Arend. 2017. "Contribution of Services to Economic Growth: Kaldor's Fifth Law?" *RAM. Revista de Administração Mackenzie* 18, no. 4: 190–213.

Goldman, Eric. 1952. *Rendezvous with Destiny: A History of Modern American Reform*. New York: Knopf.

Gordon, Peter-John. 2019. "Education Financing: Who Should Pay, and Why?" *Jamaica Observer*. 17 September. http://m.jamaicaobserver.com/opinion/education-financing -who-should-pay-and-why-_172598?profile=1096.

Haigh, Martin J. 2002. "Internationalisation of the Curriculum: Designing Inclusive Education for a Small World". *Journal of Geography in Higher Education* 26, no. 1: 49–66.

Handy, C. 1993. *Understanding Organizations*. 4th ed. London: Penguin.

Harriott, Anthony A., Balford A. Lewis, Kenisha V. Nelson and Mitchell A. Seligson. 2013. "Political Culture of Democracy in Jamaica and in the Americas, 2012: Towards Equality of Opportunity". *USAID*. March 2013. https://www.vanderbilt.edu/lapop/ jamaica/Jamaica_Country_Report_2012_W.pdf.

Hart-Davis, Adam. 2015. *History: From the Dawn of Civilization to the Present Day*. London: D.K. Publishing.

Healey, Nigel. 2015. "Universities That Set Up Branch Campuses in Other Countries Are Not Colonisers". *Conversation*. 19 October. http://theconversation.com/universities -that-set-up-branch-campuses-in-other-countries-are-not-colonisers-46289.

HEART/NTA. 2009. "Unattached Youth in Jamaica". https://www.mona.uwi.edu/cop /sites/default/files/Unattached%20youth_0.pdf.

Heatherfield, Susan M. 2018. "Leadership Vision: You Can't Be a Real Leader Who People Want to Follow Without Vision". *Balance Careers*. Last modified 6 March 2019. https://www.thebalancecareers.com/leadership-vision-1918616.

Hecht, Ben. 2013. "Collaboration Is the New Competition". *Harvard Business Review*. 10 January. https://hbr.org/2013/01/collaboration-is-the-new-compe.

Hewitt, Dundee D. 2012. *The Teachers' Struggles Continue: A Critical Analysis of the Contributions of Teachers' Unions and Selected Educators from 1894–2012*. Kingston: Jamaica Publishing House.

Heywood, Norman, and Michael Lawrence. 2014. "Youth Victimisation and Offending in Jamaica: An Analysis of Serious Violent Crimes". Study commissioned by the Research, Planning and Legal Services Branch of the Jamaica Constabulary Force.

Holten-Andersen, Per. 2015. "The Role of Universities in Modern Societies". https://www.cbs.dk/en/about-cbs/organisation/senior-management/news/the-role-of-universities-in-modern-societies. Accessed 3 April 2020.

Hurley, Robert. 2006. "The Decision to Trust". *Harvard Business Review*. https://hbr.org/2006/09/the-decision-to-trust. Accessed 30 June 2017.

Hutchinson-Jafar, Linda. 2015. "No Clear Winner Projected in Trinidad Election". *Reuters*. 7 September. https://www.reuters.com/article/us-trinidadtobago-election/no-clear-winner-projected-in-trinidad-election-idUSKCN0R70BV20150907.

Itam, Samuel, Simon Cueva, Erik Lundback, Janet Stotsky and Stephen Tokarick. 2000. "Developments and Challenges in the Caribbean Region". *International Monetary Fund Publications Paper 201*. 31 December. https://www.imf.org/external/pubs/nft/op/201/.

Jamaica Information Service. 2004. "The UWI Grapples with the Impact of WTO/GATS on the Higher Education Sector in the Region". 27 April. https://jis.gov.jm/the-uwi-grapples-with-the-impact-of-wtogats-on-the-higher-education-sector-in-the-region/.

Jessen, Anneke, and Ennio Rodriguez. 1999. *The Caribbean Community: Facing the Challenges of Regional and Global Integration*. InterAmerican Development Bank Occasional Paper 2. January. https://publications.iadb.org/en/publication/10893/caribbean-community-facing-challenges-regional-and-global-integration.

Johnson, Jovan. 2017. "Government Clueless! More Than $1 Billion Spent Training Workers but No System in Place to Assess Benefit". *Gleaner*. 8 March. http://jamaica-gleaner.com/article/lead-stories/20170308/government-clueless-more-1-billion-spent-training-workers-no-system.

Jones, Ian. 2018. "Top Ten Most Productive Countries – 2018 List". *Gazette Review*. https://gazettereview.com/2016/05/the-ten-most-productive-countries/.

Jones, Ken. 2014. "Remedying Voter Apathy". *Gleaner*. 19 January. http://jamaica-gleaner.com/gleaner/20140119/focus/focus1.html.

Jones, Sara, and Stephen Clulow. 2012. "How to Foster a Culture of Collaboration between Universities and Industry". *Guardian*. 2 August. https://www.theguardian.com/higher-education-network/blog/2012/aug/02/the-value-of-research-collaborations.

Kenny, John. 2008. "Efficiency and Effectiveness in Higher Education. Who Is Accountable for What?" https://files.eric.ed.gov/fulltext/EJ802278.pdf.

Killick, David. 2014. *Developing the Global Student: Higher Education in an Era of Globalization*. Abingdon: Routledge.

Kirton, Raymond Mark, Marlon Anatol and Niki Braithwaite. 2010. "The Political Culture of Democracy in Trinidad and Tobago: Democracy in Action, Inter-American Development Bank, Trinidad". https://www.vanderbilt.edu/lapop/trinidad-tobago/2010-political-culture.pdf. Accessed 3 April 2020.

Knight, Jane. 2014. "Three Generations of Cross-Border Higher Education: New Developments, Issues and Challenges". In *Internationalisation of Higher Education and Global Mobility*, edited by Bernhard T. Streitwieser, 43–58. Didcot, UK: Symposium Books.

Knight, Jane, and Hans de Wit. 1999. *Quality and Recognized Internationalization in Higher Education*. Paris: OECD.

Kosmützky, Anna, and Rahul Putty. 2016. "Transcending Borders and Traversing Boundaries: A Systematic Review of the Literature on Transnational, Offshore, Cross-Border, and Borderless Higher Education". *Journal of Studies in International Education* 20, no. 1: 8–33.

Kruk, Edward. 2012. "Father Absence, Father Deficit, Father Hunger: The Vital Importance of Paternal Presence in Children's Lives". *Psychology Today*. https://www.psychologytoday.com/intl/blog/co-parenting-after-divorce/201205/father-absence-father-deficit-father-hunger.

Kumari, Reenu, and Anil Kumar Sharma. 2017. "Determinants of Foreign Direct Investment in Developing Countries: A Panel Data Study". *International Journal of Emerging Markets* 12, no. 4: 658–82. https://doi.org/10.1108/IJoEM-10-2014-0169.

Kuper, Adam. 1976. *Changing Jamaica*. London: Routledge and Kegan Paul.

Levy, Horace. 2019. "Social Intervention, Regular Policing Crucial to Solving Crime Problem". http://jamaica-gleaner.com/article/commentary/20190510/horace-levy-social-intervention-regular-policing-crucial-solving-crime.

Lewis, Henry J. 2018. "The Business of Funding Tertiary Education". *Jamaica Observer*. 24 April. http://www.jamaicaobserver.com/opinion/the-business-of-funding-tertiary-education_131362?profile=1096.

Litman, Todd. 2013. "Principles of Effective Planning". https://www.vtpi.org/planning.pdf.

Looker, Ian. 2018. "What Are the Challenges Facing Higher Education in 2018?" 31 January. https://pwc.blogs.com/publicsectormatters/2018/01/what-are-the-challenges-facing-higher-education-in-2018.html.

Ma, Wan-hua. 2003. "Economic Reform and Higher Education in China". CIDE Occasional Papers Series, Los Angeles: Center for International and Development Education. http://www.usp.br/feafuturo/assets/files/China.pdf.

Malin, Joel R., and Christopher Lubienski. 2015. "Educational Expertise, Advocacy, and Media Influence". *Education Policy Analysis Archives* 23, no. 6: 1–32. https://epaa.asu.edu/ojs/article/viewFile/1706/1456.

Mandela, Nelson. 2018. *The Prison Letters of Nelson Mandela*. New York: Liveright Publishing.

Manley, Michael. 1983. *Jamaica, Struggle in the Periphery*. London: Third World Media, in association with Writers and Readers Publishing Cooperative Society.

———. 1987. *Up the Down Escalator: Development and the International Economy: A Jamaican Case Study*. Washington, DC: Howard University Press.

Mattoo, Aaditya. 2000. "Developing Countries in the New Round of GATS Negotiations: Towards a Pro-active Role". *World Economy* 23, no. 4: 471–89.

Maxwell, Joseph A. 1998. "Designing a Qualitative Study". In *Handbook of Applied Social Research Methods*, edited by Leonard Bickman and Debra J. Rog, 69–100. Thousand Oaks, CA: Sage.

Mayer, R.C., J.J. Davis and F.D. Schoorman. 1995. "An Integrative Model of Organizational Trust". *Academy of Management Review* 20, no. 3: 709–34.

McKeachie, Wilbert J. 2002. *Teaching Tips: Strategies, Research, and Theory for College and University Teachers*. Boston: Houghton Mifflin Company.

McLaughlin, Maureen. 2003. "Tertiary Education Policy in New Zealand". https://www.fulbright.org.nz/wp-content/uploads/2011/12/axford2002_mclaughlin.pdf.

Morgan, William J., and Bin Wu. 2011. *Higher Education Reform in China: Beyond the Expansion*. Abingdon, UK: Routledge.

Munroe, Trevor. 1972. *The Politics of Constitutional Decolonization*. Kingston: Institute of Social and Economic Research, University of the West Indies.

Nettleford, Rex M. 1970. *Mirror, Mirror*. London, England, and Kingston, Jamaica: Collins and Sangster.

New Zealand Government. 2014. "Tertiary Education Strategy 2014–2019". http://www.education.govt.nz/further-education/policies-and-strategies/tertiary-education-strategy/.

Nicholas, Arlene. 2008. "Preferred Learning Methods of the Millennial Generation". Faculty and Staff Publications, no. 15. 10.18848/1447-9494/CGP/v15i06/45805.

Oblinger, Diana. 2003. "Boomers, Gen-Xers, and Millennials: Understanding the 'New Students'". *EDUCAUSE Review* 500, no. 4: 37–47.

OECD. 2017. "Fostering Innovation in the Public Sector". https://oecd-opsi.org/wp-content/uploads/2018/07/Fostering-Innovation-in-the-Public-Sector-254-pages.pdf.

Office of the Contractor General. 2017. "Special Report of Investigation into the Award of Contracts for the Island-Wide Mitigation (De-Bushing and Drain Cleaning) Programme which Was Implemented by the National Works Agency (NWA) in the Amount of Six Hundred and Six Million Dollars". http://ocg.gov.jm/ocg/investigation-reports/special-report-investigation-award-contracts-island-wide-mitigation-de-bushing.

Okech, Benson Benedict. 2017. "Value for Money in Provision of Services in the Public Sector of Uganda". *Texila International Journal of Management* 3, no. 2 (November): 118–30. https://www.texilajournal.com/thumbs/article/Management_Vol%203 _Issue%202_Article_12.pdf.

Pazzanese, Christina. 2017. "The Challenges Facing Higher Ed". *Harvard Gazette*. 26 April. https://news.harvard.edu/gazette/story/2017/04/excellence-access-and-affordability -top-concerns-for-higher-ed-faust-says/.

Pena, Samantha. 2017. "What Is Courageous Leadership". *Creator*. 14 June. https://www .wework.com/creator/how-to-guides/what-is-courageous-leadership/.

Polka, Walter. 2018. "How and Why This Leadership Research Commenced and So What?" Preface to *7 Deadly Sins on Leadership*, 1–11. 21 April. https://dailypost .niagara.edu/.../A.-Preface-to-Book-on-7-Deadly-Sins-in-Leadership/. Accessed 13 October 2018.

Posner, Barry Z., and James M. Kouzes. 1988. "Relating Leadership and Credibility". *Psychological Reports* 63, no. 2: 527–30.

Pratt, Jonathan, Steve Matthews, Bruce Nairne, Elizabeth Hoult and Stuart Ashenden. 2011. "Collaboration Between Universities: An Effective Way of Sustaining Community-University Partnerships?" *Gateways: International Journal of Community Research and Engagement* 4:119–35.

Prensky, Marc. 2001. "Digital Natives, Digital Immigrants". *On the Horizon* 9, no. 5: 1–6.

Radcliffe, Brent. 2019. "How Education and Training Affect the Economy". https:// www.investopedia.com/articles/economics/09/education-training-advantages.asp.

Rawls, J.L. 1999. "Faculty-Administration Conflict: Bridging the Gap for Collaborative Leadership in Higher Education". Typescript.

Reitz, Charles. 2016. *Philosophy and Critical Pedagogy: Insurrection and Commonwealth*. Bern, Switzerland: Peter Lang.

Remler, Dahlia. 2016. "Are 90% of Academic Papers Really Never Cited? Reviewing the Literature on Academic Citations". *LSE Impact Blog*. 1 November. http://blogs .lse.ac.uk/impactofsocialsciences/2014/04/23/academic-papers-citation-rates -remler/.

Robertson, Roland. 1992. *Globalization: Social Theory and Global Culture*. London: Sage.

Sandiford, Robert Edison. 2018. "Barbados Elects First Female PM in Opposition Landslide". *Reuters*. 25 May. https://www.reuters.com/article/us-barbados-election /barbados-elects-first-female-pm-in-opposition-landslide-idUSKCN1IQ1N3.

Santiago, Paulo, Karine Tremblay, Ester Basri and Elena Arnal. 2008. "Tertiary Education for a Knowledge Society". *Synthesis Report on OECD Thematic Review of Tertiary Education*. http://www.oecd.org/education/skills-beyond-school/40345176 .pdf.

Sauvé, Pierre. 2002. "Trade, Education and the GATS: What's In, What's Out, What's All the Fuss About?" *Higher Education Management and Policy* 14, no. 3: 47–76.

Sen, Amartya. 2002. "Globalization: Past and Present". *Ishizaka Lectures.Tokyo, Japan.* 18 February.

Senge, Peter M. 1990. *The Fifth Discipline: The Art and Practice of the Learning Organization.* New York: Doubleday/Currency. https://files.eric.ed.gov/fulltext/EJ802278.pdf and http://infed.org/mobi/peter-senge-and-the-learning-organization/.

Shepherd, Verene. 2018. "Rodney's Impact on Academia and Activism". *Gleaner.* 17 October. http://jamaica-gleaner.com/article/commentary/20181017/verene -shepherd-rodneys-impact-academia-and-activism.

Sickler, S.M. 2009. "A Study of Millennial Student Learning Preferences: An Analysis of Two Interior Design Class Case Studies". http://fsu.digital.flvc.org/islandora /object/fsu%3A176230. Accessed 3 April 2020.

Slutkin, Gary. 2013. "Contagion of Violence: Workshop Summary". *Violence Is a Contagious Disease.* 6 February. https://www.ncbi.nlm.nih.gov/books/NBK207245/.

Stewart, Alston, ed. 2019. "Securing a Safer Jamaica". Report from the National Crime and Violence Prevention Summit. July.

Study International. 2018. "Which Country Is Home to the Largest International Student Population?" https://www.studyinternational.com/news/country-home -largest-international-student-population/.

Suárez-Orozco, Marcelo, and D. Boalian Qin-Hilliard. 2004. *Globalization: Culture and Education in the New Millennium.* Berkeley: University of California Press.

Symonds, Quacquarelli. 2017. "Developing World Leads in Student Population Growth". https://www.qs.com/developing-world-leads-in-student-population-growth/

Tardanico, Sandra. 2013. "10 Traits of Courageous Leaders". *Forbes.* 15 January. https:// www.forbes.com/sites/susantardanico/2013/01/15/10-traits-of-courageous-leaders /#13a48d764fc0.

Thompson, Canute. S. 2009. *Towards Solutions: Fundamentals of Transformational Leadership in a Postmodern Era.* Mandeville, Jamaica: Northern Caribbean University Press.

———. 2015. "Locating the Epicentre of Effective (Educational) Leadership in the 21st Century". Caribbean Leadership Re-Imagination Initiative, Mona School of Business and Management, University of the West Indies.

———. 2017. "An Exploration of Faculty Involvement in Attitudes toward Strategic Planning in Their Institutions". *Educational Planning* 24, no. 1: 7–19.

Tilak, Jandhyala B.G. 2011. *Trade in Higher Education: The Role of the General Agreement on Trade in Services (GATS).* Paris: UNESCO.

Transparency International. 2017. "Corruption Perceptions Index 2017". Last modified 21 February 2018. https://www.libertadciudadana.org/archivos/IPC2017/CPI %202017%20Global%20Report%20English.pdf.

———. 2018. "Corruption Perceptions Index 2018". https://www.transparency.org /cpi2018.

Ubah, Charles. 2007. "Immigrants' Experiences in America: Toward Understanding Organized Crime". *African Journal of Criminology and Justice Studies* 3, no. 1: 95–118.

"Unclaimed Property in the Caribbean". *UPPO*. 29 November. https://www.uppo.org /blogpost/925381/263367/Unclaimed-property-in-the-Caribbean.

University Council of Jamaica. 2018. "Overseas Accredited and Recognized Programmes". Last modified 19 March 2019. https://www.ucj.org.jm/accreditation /overseas-accredited-and-recognised-programmes/.

University of the West Indies (UWI). 2017. "The UWI Triple A Strategy 2017–2022: Revitalizing Caribbean Development". https://sta.uwi.edu/fss/heu/sites/default /files/heu/The%20UWI%20Triple%20A%20Strategic%20Plan%202017%20 -%202022%20Full%20Plan%20.pdf.

———. 2018. "The University Office of Planning Statistical Digest 2012/13 to 2016/17: A Statistical Review of 5 Year Trends in Student Enrolment and Graduation Statistics at The UWI During the Period 2012/13 to 2016/17 for Selected Datasets". https:// www.mona.uwi.edu/principal/sites/default/files/principal/statistics/2016-2017/C .P6d%20-%20The%20UWI%20Statistical%20Digest%202012-13%20to%202016-17 .pdf.

US Department of Justice. 1990. "Jamaican Posse". *Intelligence Bulletin* 90, no. 2: 23. https://www.ncjrs.gov/App/Publications/abstract.aspx?ID=127325.

Vasciannie, Stephen. 2017. "UTech and the Question of Law". *Jamaica Observer*. 1 October. http://m.jamaicaobserver.com/news/utech-and-the-question-of-law _112237?profile=0.

Vedder, Richard. 2017. "Seven Challenges Facing Higher Education". *Forbes*. 29 August. https://www.forbes.com/sites/ccap/2017/08/29/seven-challenges-facing-higher -education/#596654553180.

Waite, Basil. 2008. "The Child Opportunity Trust Fund". Paper presented to the Parliament of Jamaica.

Walter, Ekaterina. 2015. "12 Leadership Behaviors that Build Team Trust". *Forbes*. 1 December. https://www.forbes.com/sites/ekaterinawalter/2015/12/01/12-leadership -behaviors-that-build-team-trust/#557352797221.

Ward, Elizabeth, Paris Lyew Ayee and Deanna Ashley. 2012. "The Impact of Urban Violence on Jamaican Children: Challenges and Responses". https://bernardvanleer .org/app/uploads/2015/12/ECM119_Community-violence-and-young-children -making-space-for-hope.pdf.

Wells, Ricardo. 2017. "Student Loan Debts Block Scholarships". *Tribune 242*. 16 June. http://www.tribune242.com/photos/2017/jun/16/49068/.

White, Garth. 1967. "Rudie, Oh Rudie!" *Caribbean Quarterly* 13, no. 3: 39–44.

Williams, Carl. 2007. "Consequences of the War on Drugs for Transit Countries: The Jamaican Experience". *Crime and Justice International* 23 (September–October): 31–38.

———. 2015. "The Long Arm of the Law: Bringing International Drug Offenders to Justice in American Courts". *Beijing Law Review* 6:102–16. http://dx.doi.org/10.4236 /blr.2015.61011.

Williams, Carl, and Mitchel P. Roth. 2011. "The Importation and Re-exportation of Organized Crime: Explaining the Rise and Fall of the Jamaican Posses in the United States". *Trends in Organized Crime* 14:298–313.

Williams, Densil. 2019. "More Prosperity, More Poverty". *Gleaner*. 25 August. http:// jamaica-gleaner.com/article/focus/20190825/densil-williams-more-prosperity-more -poverty.

Williams, Eric Eustace. 1970. *From Columbus to Castro: The History of the Caribbean, 1492–1969*. London: Deutsch.

———. 1944. *Capitalism and Slavery*. North Carolina: University of North Carolina Press.

World Bank. 2017. "World Bank Country and Lending Groups". https://datahelpdesk .worldbank.org/knowledgebase/articles/906519-world-bank-country-and-lending -groups.

———. 2019. "The World Bank in Jamaica". https://www.worldbank.org/en/country /jamaica/overview. Accessed 3 April 2020.

———. n.d. "School Enrollment, Tertiary (% Gross) – Jamaica". https://data.worldbank .org/indicator/se.ter.enrr. Accessed 3 April 2020.

World Economic Forum. 2015a. "How Does Corruption Affect Economic Growth?" https://www.weforum.org/agenda/2015/05/how-does-corruption-affect-economic -growth/.

———. 2015b. "The Human Capital Report 2015". http://www3.weforum.org/docs /WEF_Human_Capital_Report_2015.pdf.

World Population Review. 2019. "Murder Rate by Country". http://worldpopulation review.com/countries/murder-rate-by-country/.

Wu, Di. 2006. "Analyzing China's Automobile Industry Competitiveness through Porter's Diamond Model". Open ULeth Scholarship. https://hdl.handle.net/10133 /583.

Wynter, Brian. 2011. "Productivity in Jamaica". Speech. 13 September. http://boj.org.jm /uploads/news/speech_-_jcc_luncheon,_2011-9-13.pdf.

Zhou, Mi, and Louis Vaccaro. 2007. "Strengthening the Relationship between Higher Education and Regional Economic Development". Semantic Scholar. https://api .semanticscholar.org/CorpusID:10183344.

Index

Page numbers in italics refer to figures and tables.

absence of fathers, 84

abusive mother–son relationships, 83

accountability: courageous leaders, 122; impeachment and, 100–103; public sector, 110

activism, 6–7, 47–54; decline in, 51; history, 47, 48; social media, 47, 52; student, 51–52; teachers, 52

Adams, Tom, 90

Adventist Church, 79

Africa, 28, 60, 89

Albania, 18

Alexander the Great, 14

Allaire, Jason, 20

Allen, Erica, 76

Allied Workers Union, 50

Al-Rodhan, Nayef, 14

Altbach, Philip G., 14, 16, 24

Anatol, Marlon, 92

Anti-Gang Strategy of the Jamaica Constabulary Force, 79, 80

Antigua and Barbuda: dormant bank accounts, 43; elections and voters turnout, 91–92; political tendencies, 90; tertiary participation rate, 42

Antigua and Barbuda Labour Party, 91–92

Arend, Marcelo, 62

Asamoah, Sam Rockson, 64

Ashley, Deanna, 71, 84, 85

Asian Productivity Organization, 60; Productivity Databook, 36, 60

Asian Productivity Report, 59, 61

Atlanta, 25–26

at-risk youths, 80; characteristics, 76; diversion programmes, 80; isolation, 77; re-socialization, 77; violence and, 76–77. *See also* unattached youth

Australia, 18, 22, 30, 31

Azerbaijan, 18

Bahamas, 4, 5, 18, 42, 43, 72, 90, 95, 97

Bank of Jamaica, 63

Bar Association, 81

Barbados: activism, 9; borderlessness, 18; corruption, 4, 95, 97; dormant bank accounts, 43; enrolment decline, 41, 42; financing higher education, 42; leadership, 8–9, 89, 90; as an outlier, 42; racism and social stratification, 8–9; voter turnout, 91

Barrow, Errol, 8, 9, 89, 90

Barrow, John, 104

Barrows, Nita, 49

Bass, Bernard M., 93–94

Beckford, George, 49, 50, 61

Beckles, Hilary, 49

Belarus, 18

Belize, 5, 5, 42, 72, 98

Bernal, Richard, 20, 89–90

Bird, Lester, 90

Bird, Vere, 90

Blanchard, Kenneth, 93, 97

Boham, Hector, 64

borderlessness, 16–18
Braithwaite, Niki, 92
Brathwaite, Kamau, 49
Brazil, 60, 62, *73*, 100
Brexit, 90
BRICS (Brazil, Russia, India, China and South Africa), 60
British colonies, 4
Browne, Gaston, 91–92
Bullock, Colin, 119
Bunting, Peter, 70
Burnham, Forbes, 90
Burrowes, Keith, 96, 97, 103

Callaghan, Brett, 8
Calmera, Runy, 3
Cammaerts, Bart, 47
Canada, 17, 29, 31, 62
Capitalism and Slavery (Williams), 8
Caribbean: activism, 6–7, 47–54; corruption, 4–5, 64–65, 94–95; crime, 4, 5, 70–86; issues facing, 3–5; power and leadership, 5–9; public trust, 96–103. *See also* higher education/higher education institutions (HEIs); *and specific countries*
Caribbean Examinations Council, 68
Caribbean Policy Research Institute (CaPRI), 34–35, 36, 40, 41
Cave Hill Campus in Barbados, 41
Central Bank, 43
challenges facing higher education, 20–21
Chanda, Rupa, 14
Changing Jamaica (Kuper), 50–51
Charles, Eugenia, 49
Chi, Wei, 68
chief justice, appointment of, 6–7
Child Abuse Mitigation Project, 84
Children First, 84

Child Resiliency Programme, 84
Child Trust Fund, 39–40
China, 31, 36–38, 60; Caribbean presence, 89–90; economy and education, 37, 66–67; enrolment ratio, 36; as fastest-growing economy, 67; GDP growth in, 37, 67; graduate population, 68; higher education institutions (HEIs), 36–37; higher education market and, 20; international student population, 29, 30, 31; labour market, 68; labour productivity, 60; property rights, 66; technical and vocational education, 36
China Policy Institute, University of Nottingham, 68
Chinese workforce, 36
Civil Service Establishment, 109
Clansman Gang, 79
Clarke, Colin, 79
Clarke, Nigel, 64
Clulow, Stephen, 26
Coleman, David, 17
collaboration. *See* inter-institutional partnerships
Collier, Paul, 14–15
Collins, J., 3
Colombia, 72
colonialism, 9, 15
commercial banks, unclaimed assets in, 43
Commonwealth, 104–5, 107
communal trust, 96
competition, 30–32
The Conversation, 48
Coombs, Michael, 84
Córdova, José, 59
corruption, 4–5, 91; economic growth and, 64–65; election campaign

spending, 65; problem of, 94–95; recommendations to curb, 65

Corruption Perception Index, 95

Corruption Prevention and Integrity Commission (CPIC), 101–2

courageous leadership, 118–23; concept, 118; cowardism and, 120–21, 122; forms, 118; traits, 121–23

Court of Appeal, 102, 113

COVID-19 pandemic, 67

cowardism, 120–21, 122

craft vending, 62

crime, 4, 5, 70–86; at-risk and unattached youth, 77–79; dealing with, 76–77; disease control model, 76–77, 83; murders, 73–75; political parties and gangs, 79–82; root causes, 75–85; statistics, 72, 72–73; weak family systems and, 83–85; Zones of Special Operations, 85. *See also* gangs

Cross-Border Education Research Team at State University of New York, 18–19

Csiszar, John, 58

cultural advocacy, 50

cultural assimilation, 14

culture of reasonableness, 111–15

currency devaluation, 63–64

David Simmonds Tivoli Commission of Inquiry report, 80

Davis, Carlton, 104–6

Davis, J.J., 6

della Porta, Donnatella, 47

de Moll, K. E., 6

dentistry programmes, 38

dentist-to-patient ratio, 38

devaluation of Jamaican dollar, 63–64

de Wit, Hans, 16

Diani, Mario, 47

Dicken, Peter, 14

digitizing public records, 115

disease control model, 76–77, 83

divide-and-rule tactics, 52

Dollar, David, 14–15

dollar, devaluation of, 63–64

domestic market, liberalization of, 13–14. *See also* General Agreement on Trade in Services (GATS)

Dominica, 4, 5, 42, 73, 95

Dominican Republic, 73

dormant bank accounts, 43

Drori, Gili S., 22

drugs, 81–82

Dujon, Daryl, 3

Duncan, Joan, 109

Duncan-Scott, Donna, 109

East Kingston gangs, 79

Economic Club of Washington DC, 20–21

economic growth, 55–69; corruption and, 64–65; craft vending, 62; devaluation of currency, 63–64; GDP, 55, 56–57, 57, 61, 65, 95; higher education and, 66–69; macroeconomic stability, 58–60; measurements, 57–58; productivity profile compared, 60–61; service sector, 61–62; trade deficit, 61; US dollar debt, 63

economic recession of 2007–8, 25

"Economic Reform and Higher Education in China" (Ma), 66

"Education Attainment and the Labour Market in China, 1989–2013" (Chi, Freeman, and Li), 68

Education City in Doha, 18

Edwards, Al, 94

Elections and Boundaries Commission of Trinidad and Tobago, 91

Electoral Commission of Jamaica, 90

Ellington, Owen, 70, 73–74, 75

El Salvador, 72

engaging entrepreneurship. *See* entrepreneurship

English language, 22

enrolments. *See* student enrolments

entrepreneurial university, 32–33. *See also* entrepreneurship

entrepreneurship, 58; Chinese economy, 37, 66, 67; craft, 62; universities, 32–33, 34, 35

European Union, 18, 32

exploitation of workers, 52

fatherless children, 84

Faust, Drew Gilpin, 18, 35–36, 37, 48

fearlessness, 122

feedback, 122

feminist movement, 51

feminist theology, 51

financing higher education, 34–43; approaches to, 38–43; CaPRI, 34–35, 36, 40, 41; Child Trust Fund, 39–40; industry-alignment Chinese model, 36–38; market model, 40–41

Finland, 62, 65

first-generation gangs, 73–74. *See also* gangs

flipped classroom, 29

foreign direct investment, 3, 15, 65

"Fostering Innovation in the Public Sector" (OECD), 116

fourth-generation gangs, 74. *See also* gangs

France, 51, 52, 100

Frater, Terence, 22

Freeman, Richard, 68

From Columbus to Castro: The History of the Caribbean, 1492–1969 (Williams), 8

Galbraith, J. K., 6

gangs: criminal, 74, 80; displaced, 82–83; generations, 73–74; guns, drugs and, 81–82; murders and, 73–75; neutralization, 75; number, 79; political parties and, 79–82; social conditions and, 75–77. *See also* crime

Gayle (criminologist), 70–71, 72, 74–75, 76, 80, 83–84, 85

Gazette Review, 62

GDP. *See* gross domestic product (GDP)

General Agreement on Trade in Services (GATS), 13–24; actions for contending with, 23–24; features, 24; globalization and, 15–21, 24; structure and history, 13–15; UWI and, 21–24

Generation Z, 30

Germany, 30–31

Giovanini, Adilson, 62

GlaxoSmithKline, 26

Gleaner, 75, 81, 119–20

Global Corruption Barometer, 96–97

Global Engagement and Research at StudyPortals, 24

globalization, 14–21, 24; as cultural-political project, 14; first wave, 14; second phase, 15; third phase, 15

glocalization, 22–23

Goede, Miguel, 3

Golding, Bruce, 79

Golding, Mark, 64

Goldman, Eric, 93

Gordon, Peter-John, 40–41

Government of India. *See* India

Great Britain. *See* United Kingdom

Greek civilization, 14

Grey, Lord, 104, 105

Groningen Growth and Development Centre, 61–62

gross domestic product (GDP): China, 37, 67; India, 60–61; Jamaica, 55, 56–57, 57, 61, 65, 95; labour productivity and, 60–61; Mexico, 59. *See also* economic growth

"Group Executive Director of Culture and Human Development," 109

Guatemala, 72

Guiding Framework for Entrepreneurial Universities (OECD), 32–33

guns/gun crime, 73; gangs, drugs and, 81–82

Guyana, 4, 42, 49, 90, 98

Guyana Chronicle, 103

Haigh, Martin J., 19

Haiti, 95

Handy, C., 6

Harriott, Anthony A., 70, 72, 98

Hecht, Ben, 25–26

Hewitt, Dundee D., 54

Heywood, Norman, 77

higher education/higher education institutions (HEIs), 13–33; borderlessness, 16–18; CaPRI, 34–35, 36, 40, 41; challenges facing, 20–21; competition, 30–32; demand growth, 28–29; diversifying products and delivery pathways, 27–33; economic growth and, 66–69; enrolments, 21, 31, 31–32, 36, 37, 41–42; entrepreneurship, 32–33, 34, 35; financing, 34–43; inclusive approach to strategic planning, 24–33; inter-institutional partnerships, 17–18, 25–26; internationalization, 19–20; millennials and, 30; quality assurance with speed and efficiency, 26–27; technological solutions, 29–30; "Think Tertiary Early" approach, 36,

39; unbounded university model, 29–30

"Historic Rates of the Jamaican Dollar to the US Dollar" report (Bank of Jamaica), 63

Höllerer, Markus A., 22

Holness, Andrew, 63

Honduras, 72, 73

"How Does Corruption Affect Economic Growth?", 64

"How Education and Training Affect the Economy" (Radcliffe), 67–68

Human Capital Leveraging Index, 62

Human Employment and Resource Training Trust (HEART), 78

Hurley, Robert, 6

Hutchinson-Jafar, Linda, 91

IBIS World, 58

illicit drugs, 81

immigration policies, 82

impeachment, 100–103, 118

India, 31, 100; GDP growth, 60–61; higher education in, 35–36; higher education market and, 20; labour productivity, 60–61; services and skill development, 60

Indonesia, 31

Industrial Disputes Tribunal (IDT), 111–15

information and communication technology (ICT)-driven economy, 20

innovation in public sector, 116–17

Integrity Commission, 102

Inter-American Development Bank, 55

inter-institutional partnerships, 17–18, 25–26

internationalization, 14, 24; higher education, 15, 16, 19–20, 22, 25; University of the West Indies (UWI), 22

International Monetary Fund, 5, 55, 63, 65

international students: business expansion for HEIs, 28; enrolment, *31*, 31–32; fees/income from, 19, 21; market for, 24, 29; population, 29, 30–31; United Kingdom and, 21; UWI and, 22, 24, *31*, 31–32

Ireland, 100

Jagan, Cheddie, 90

Jamaica: Child Trust Fund, 39–40; crime, 5, 70–86; dentist-to-patient ratio, 38; economic growth, 55–69; illicit drugs, 81; political independence, 70; as transit zone for drugs, 81; tuition for several final-year students, 41–42. *See also* higher education/higher education institutions (HEIs); public sector

Jamaica Civil Service Association, 110

Jamaica Constabulary Force, 74, 75, 79, 80

Jamaica Defence Force, 78

Jamaica Information Service (JIS), 22

Jamaica Labour Party, 63

Jamaica Money Market Brokers Group, 109

Jamaican Bar Association, 7

Jamaican dollars. *See* dollar, devaluation of

Jamaica Observer, 63, 64, 105

Jamaica Teachers' Association (JTA), 53; shortcomings, 54; wage negotiations, 53–54

Japan, 15, 30, 31, 62

Jessen, Anneke, 3

Johnson, Jovan, 110

Jones, Sara, 26

Jones, Wayne, 110

Kenny, John, 27

Kirton, Raymond Mark, 92

Knight, Jane, 14, 16, 24

Kosmützky, Anna, 16–17

Kruk, Edward, 84, 85

Kumari, Reenu, 35, 36

Kuper, Adam, 50–51

Labour Relations and Industrial Disputes Act, 112, 115

Latin America, 28, 29, 51, 81, 92; Global Corruption Barometer report on, 96–97; murder per capita, 72–73

Latin America Public Opinion Project, 92, 98

law programmes, 38

Lawrence, Michael, 77

leadership: courageous, 118–23; developing and demonstrating, 93–94; nation-states founders, 89; power and, 5–9; voting patterns, 90–93. *See also* public trust

Leading at a Higher Level (Blanchard), 93

Learning, Earning, Giving Back and Saving (LEGS), 78, 86

Levy, Horace, 70–71, 72, 76, 80

Lewis, Arthur, 49

Lewis, Henry J., 34, 35, 36

Li, Hongbin, 68

liberalization, 13–14. *See also* General Agreement on Trade in Services (GATS)

Litman, Todd, 25

Local Improvements (Communities Amenities) Act, 81

Looker, Ian, 21

Lubienski, Christopher, 1, 48

Lyew Ayee, Paris, 71, 84, 85

Ma, Wan-hua, 66–67
macroeconomic stability, 58–60
Mair, Lucille Mathurin, 49
Malin, Joel R., 1, 48
Manley, Michael, 90
Manley, Norman, 8, 9, 89, 90
"March for Our Lives," 51–52
market model of Gordon, 40–41
Marx, Karl, 52, 54
Matthews Lane gangs, 79, 82
Mattis, General, 119
Mattoo, Aaditya, 13–14
Maxwell, Joseph A., 93
Mayer, R. C., 6
McKeachie, Wilbert J., 30
McKendrick, John, 94
McLaughlin, Maureen, 36, 38, 39
Mexico: economic growth, 59;
    macroeconomic stability, 59; murder
    rate, 73
millennials, 30
Mirror Mirror (Nettleford), 49
money, value for, 109–10
Mongolia, 60
"More Prosperity, More Poverty," 67
Morgan, William J., 68
movements. *See* activism
Munroe, Trevor, 49, 50
murders, 5, 5, 73–75; gun-related, 73;
    political violence and, 73. *See also* crime
Myanmar, 60

National Commercial Bank (NCB),
    112–13, 114
National Crime and Violence
    Prevention Summit, 71, 72, 78
National Integrity Action, 50
National Service Enlistment, 78
National Unattached Youth Programme,
    78, 86

National Works Agency, 121
Nettleford, Rex, 49, 50
New York University, 18–19
New Zealand, 22, 36, 38–39, 65
Nicholas, Arlene, 30
non-aligned movement, 89
North America, 51
North American Free Trade A
    greement, 59
North Atlantic Treaty Organization, 15
Norway, 62

Oblinger, Diana, 30
One Order Gang, 79
online learning, 20, 29, 41
Open Campus enrolments, 41
Organisation for Economic
    Co-operation and Development
    (OECD), 15, 32, 116, 117
organized crime, 74
Overseas Farm Work Programme, 121
Oxford Business Group, 91

Padilla, Juan, 59
Pakistan, 31
Panama, *73*
partnerships. *See* inter-institutional
    partnerships
Pazzanese, Christina, 20–21
Peace Management Initiative, 76
Pena, Samantha, 118, 119
People's National Movement, 8, 91
People's National Party, 8, 70, 79, 82
People's Partnership Coalition, 91
performance management, 110–11
permanent secretary, 104–7, 119, 121
Persistent Poverty (Beckford), 49, 61
Pfizer, 26
Philippines, 100
Phillips, Peter, 63–64, 75, 78, 120

Philosophy and Critical Pedagogy: Insurrection and Commonwealth (Reitz), 52
Pindling, Lyndon, 90
Planning Institute of Jamaica, 55, 57, 67
political leadership. *See* leadership
political parties and gangs, 79–82
political subjugation, 52
The Politics of Constitutional Decolonization (Munroe), 50
power and leadership, 5–9
Pratt, Jonathan, 26
Prensky, Marc, 30
Presidential Click, 79
Privy Council, 7, 111–12, 113, 114, 115
Productivity Databook of Asian Productivity Organization, 36, 60
"Productivity in Jamaica" (Wynter), 60
Productivity in Mexico: Trends, Drivers and Institutional Framework, 59
property rights, 36, 66, 81
protests. *See* activism
Public Administration and Appropriations Committee, 105
public funds, misuse/waste of, 101
public officials. *See* public sector; public trust
public records, digitizing, 115
public sector, 3–4, 104–17; accountability, 110; bureaucracy, 4; culture of reasonableness, 111–15; digitizing public records, 115; innovation, 116–17; performance management, 110–11; respect for rule of law, 111–15; return on investment, 110; steps to, 107–9; as a tool, 96; value for money, 109–10. *See also* corruption
public trust, 96–103; dimensions to, 96; impeachment, 100–103
Putty, Rahul, 16–17

Qin-Hilliard, D. Boalian, 16
quality assurance standards, 26–27

racism, 8–9
Radcliffe, Brent, 67–68
Ramphal, Shridath, 49–50
Rawls, J. L., 20
Reagan, Ronald, 9
reasonableness, culture of, 111–15
Regional Negotiating Machinery, 21
Reitz, Charles, 52, 53
Remler, Dahlia, 2, 48
Research Base, 28
re-socialization of youth, 77
respect for rule of law, 111–15
Revenue Protection Division, 65
right-wing extremism, 89–90
Robertson, Roland, 22
Rodney, Walter, 49, 50
Rodriguez, Ennio, 3
Roosevelt, Teddy, 93
Roth, Mitchel P., 79, 82
Rowley, Keith, 91
rule of law: protection and preservation, 7; respect for, 111–15
Russia, 18, 29, 31, 60, 100

Samuda, Karl, 81
Santiago, Paulo, 35
School of Public Affairs of the City University of New York, 2
Schoorman, F. D., 6
Scotland, Patricia, 94
Seaga, Edward, 63
secondary schools, 53
second-generation gangs, 74. *See also* gangs
"Securing a Safer Jamaica," 71
self-government movement, 8
Sen, Amartya, 14

Senge, Peter M., 133
service sector, 13
Sewell, Audrey, 105
Sharma, Anil Kumar, 35, 36
Shepherd, Verene, 49
Singapore, 30, 31, 65
skills-leaning education system, 60
Slutkin, Gary, 71–72, 76, 77
Small Arms Survey, 73
social activism. *See* activism
social consciousness, 51, 52
Social Intervention Committee, 85
social media, 2, 4, 15, 47, 52
South Korea, 100
squatter settlements, 81
squatting, 81
Statistical Digest (UWI), 41
St Augustine Campus in Trinidad and
   Tobago, 41
Steidlmeier, Paul, 93–94
Stewart, Gordon "Butch," 91
St Kitts and Nevis, 5, 72
St Lucia, 4, 5, 42, 43, 73, 95
Stone Crusher, 79
Stoudmann, Gérard, 14
strategic planning, inclusive approach
   to, 24–33. *See also* higher education/
   higher education institutions (HEIs)
"Strengthening the Relationship
   between Higher Education and
   Regional Economic Development"
   (Zhou and Vaccaro), 37, 67
student enrolments, 21, 37; China, 36;
   decline, 41–42; international, 31, 31–32;
   New Zealand, 39; Open Campus, 41;
   UWI, 31, 31–32, 41–42
Students' Loan Bureau, 40
St Vincent and the Grenadines, 4, 5,
   73, 95
Suárez-Orozco, Marcelo, 16

Switzerland, 62
Symonds, Quacquarelli, 28

Taiwan, 30
Tardanico, Sandra, 121–22
teachers: government exploitation of,
   52–53; wage negotiations, 53–54
technological solutions, 29–30
"tell" courage leaders, 118, 119. *See also*
   courageous leadership
"Ten Fastest-Growing Industries to
   Invest in This Year" (Csiszar), 58
tertiary education. *See* higher education/
   higher education institutions (HEIs)
Tertiary Education Strategy of New
   Zealand, 38–39
Thatcher, Margaret, 9
"Think Tertiary Early" approach, 36, 39
third-generation gangs, 74. *See also* gangs
Thompson, Canute. S., 93, 94
Tilak, Jandhyala B.G., 15–16, 19, 24
Tillerson, Rex, 119
"Tivoli Invasion," 121
trade deficit, 61
trade in services, 13
transformation of public sector. *See*
   public sector
Trans-Pacific Partnership, 16
Transparency International, 4–5, 95
Trinidad and Tobago: borderlessness,
   17–18; corruption, 95, 96, 97; dormant
   bank accounts, 43; enrolment decline,
   41; lack of public trust, 96–97, 98;
   leadership, 8, 89, 90; murder rate, 5,
   72; outlier status, 42; voter turnout,
   91, 92
Triple A strategy of UWI, 22–23
Trump, D., 16, 119
trust: philosophical construction of, 6;
   public, 96–103

"trust" courage leaders, 118. *See also* courageous leadership
"try" courage leaders, 118. *See also* courageous leadership

unattached youth: crime and, 77–79; defined, 78; political strongholds and, 80, 81
unbounded university model, 29–30
unclaimed assets: commercial banks and, 43; regulations, 43
"Unclaimed Property in the Caribbean," 43
United Kingdom, 17, 21, 29, 82, 90, 104–5; activism/protests, 51, 52; Child Trust Fund, 39; higher education market dominance, 20; impeachment laws, 100; international branch campuses, 18, 21; international higher education, 31; migration to, 15; right-wing extremism, 90; universities, 21
United National Congress, 91
United Nations Children Fund, 84
United Progressive Party, 92
United States, 9, 16, 29, 90, 100, 119; anti-drug operations, 82; anti-gang operations, 82; challenges faced by HEIs, 20; displacement of gangs, 82–83; gang violence in, 82; guns/gun crime, 73; higher education market dominance, 20; immigration policies, 82; international branch campuses, 18; right-wing extremism, 90; violence in, 71
University of Brazil, 62
University of California, 26
University of Cambridge, 26
University of Southampton, 34
University of Technology, Jamaica (UTECH), 6, 38, 113, 114

University of the West Indies (UWI), 13, 17, 67; competitors of, 31; dentistry programmes, 38; enrolment, 31, 31–32, 41–42; extra-regional universities, 21; funding from regional governments, 23; GATS and, 21–24; higher education demand and, 29; internationalization, 22; law programmes, 38; multiregionality, 18; programme and course developer, 27; quality assurance process, 27; Statistical Digest, 41; strategic planning process, 25; Triple A strategy, 22–23; vocational studies/programmes, 28
US Constitution, 100
US dollars, 63

Vaccaro, Louis, 37, 67
value for money, 109–10
Vedder, Richard, 20
Venezuela, 72
violence, 70–72; anatomy of, 71–72; disease control model, 76–77, 83; political, 73; as a public health disease, 71. *See also* crime
virtual classroom, 29
voting patterns, 90–93

Waite, Basil, 40
Walgenbach, Peter, 22
Walker, Herbert, 119
Walter, Ekaterina, 93
Ward, Elizabeth, 71, 84, 85
weak family systems and crime, 83–85
Wednesbury's Law, 114
Wells, Gordon, 119–20
West Indies: integration movement, 49–50

White, Garth, 79
Williams, Carl, 70, 72, 79, 81, 82
Williams, Densil, 67
Williams, Eric, 8, 89, 91
Workers' Party of Jamaica, 50
World Bank, 28–29, 42, 55, 56, 64, 65
World Economic Forum, 64
World Finance Magazine, 58
World Health Organization (WHO), 38

World Population Review, 5
Wu, Bin, 68
Wu, Di, 36
Wynter, Brian, 60

xenophobia, 14

Zhou, Mi, 37, 67
Zones of Special Operations, 85

www.ingramcontent.com/pod-product-compliance
Lightning Source LLC
Chambersburg PA
CBHW020355270326
41926CB00007B/448